BUSINESS ETHICS

BUSINESS ETHICS

Manisha Paliwal
Associate Professor
Sinhgad Institute of Management
Pune

Publishing Globally

NEW AGE INTERNATIONAL (P) LIMITED, PUBLISHERS
New Delhi • Bangalore • Chennai • Cochin • Guwahati
Hyderabad • Kolkata • Lucknow • Mumbai
Visit us at **www.newagepublishers.com**

Published by New Age International (P) Ltd., Publishers

First Edition: 2006
Reprint: 2013

BRANCHES

- **Bangalore** 37/10, 8th Cross (Near Hanuman Temple), Azad Nagar, Chamarajpet, Bangalore-560 018
  Tel.: (080) 26756823, Telefax: 26756820, **E-mail: bangalore@newagepublishers.com**
- **Chennai** 26, Damodaran Street, T. Nagar, Chennai-600 017
  Tel.: (044) 24353401, Telefax: 24351463, **E-mail: chennai@newagepublishers.com**
- **Cochin** CC-39/1016, Carrier Station Road, Ernakulam South, Cochin-682 016
  Tel.: (0484) 2377004, Telefax: 4051303, **E-mail: cochin@newagepublishers.com**
- **Guwahati** Hemsen Complex, Mohd. Shah Road, Paltan Bazar, Near Starline Hotel, Guwahati-781 008
  Tel.: (0361) 2513881, Telefax: 2543669, **E-mail: guwahati@newagepublishers.com**
- **Hyderabad** 105, 1st Floor, Madhiray Kaveri Tower, 3-2-19, Azam Jahi Road, Nimboliadda, Hyderabad-500 027
  Tel.: (040) 24652456, Telefax: 24652457, **E-mail: hyderabad@newagepublishers.com**
- **Kolkata** RDB Chambers (Formerly Lotus Cinema) 106A, 1st Floor, S.N. Banerjee Road, Kolkata-700 014
  Tel.: (033) 22273773, Telefax: 22275247, **E-mail: kolkata@newagepublishers.com**
- **Lucknow** 16-A, Jopling Road, Lucknow-226 001
  Tel.: (0522) 2209578, 4045297, Telefax: 2204098, **E-mail: lucknow@newagepublishers.com**
- **Mumbai** 142C, Victor House, Ground Floor, N.M. Joshi Marg, Lower Parel, Mumbai-400 013
  Tel.: (022) 24927869, Telefax: 24915415, **E-mail: mumbai@newagepublishers.com**
- **New Delhi** 22, Golden House, Daryaganj, New Delhi-110 002
  Tel.: (011) 23262368, 23262370, Telefax: 43551305, **E-mail: sales@newagepublishers.com**

ISBN: 978-81-224-1855-2

₹ 150.00

C-12-09-6576

Printed in India at Ramprintograph, Delhi.
Typeset at Akarti Graphics, Delhi.

PUBLISHING FOR ONE WORLD
NEW AGE INTERNATIONAL (P) LIMITED, PUBLISHERS
7/30 A, Daryaganj, New Delhi-110002
Visit us at **www.newagepublishers.com**

Dedication

This book is dedicated to my husband Mr. Nitin Paliwal who has always been a constant source of support and encouragement to me

Foreward

The rise of the modern business organizations and global commerce has reshaped the world and has made traditional society obsolete. The mankind history has moved from hunting to barter to modern production and exchange of goods and services. Our consumer needs have exploded, technological advancements have taken place and consumer protection groups are becoming more dynamics. These profound changes gave rise to a whole range of practical theories concerning the inner functioning and organization of business activities. One of these disciplines is Business Ethics.

I am happy to note that Ms. Manisha Paliwal has exhaustively covered all the approaches having focus in protecting various interests, i.e., Social responsibility of business, Corporate Governance and Business ethics under different functional areas. The author has rightly started with the concepts of Ethics and Business ethics and the concepts of new ethics. Ethical value system and Ethical corporate behavior has been dealt in the right perspective. Equal importance hase been given to the Ethical leadership and Ethical decision making along with the ethical dilemmas in the organization. In addition to all these, Ethics in marketing, finance, human resource, information technology and Environmental ethics have been covered. Lastly Ms. Manisha has touched upon ethical issues such as Gender ethics, Sexual harassment and Discrimination.

In my view this book will be an addition to the management literature in India. It is a good source for learning, teaching and practicing managers. The book is written in a simple and lucid language, beneficial to all who are directly or indirectly involved in Business Ethics discipline.

Dr. M.M. Ali
Chairman MBA Programme
SIBER
Kolhapur (Maharashtra)

Preface

Business ethics is nothing but the application of ethics in business. It is the application of general ethical rules to business behavior. Business ethics concentrates on moral standards as they apply to business policies, institutions and behavior. It is a specialized study of moral right or wrong. It is a systematic study of ethical matters pertaining to business industry or related activities.

In any organization from top executive to bottom line employees, ethics is considered as every body' business. It is not just only achieving high level of economic performance but also to conduct one of business's most important social challenges, ethically at the same time.

Ethics in business and management is gaining momentum day by day.

The main aim of this book is to–

1. Impart knowledge, analytical skills and developments of managers to apply ethical concepts in business.
2. Introduce various ethical concepts in practical application.
3. Create awareness about moral values, corporate social responsibility.
4. Develop the abilities to resolve ethical dilemmas.
5. Inculcate high level of integrity.
6. Introduce new ethical aspects in 21st century.

I hope this book will be helpful for management students to understand the basic concepts of business ethics. As AICTE, in India has in Dec. 1995, recommended the inclusion of business ethics as a subject in management study curriculum. Therefore, many of the Indian Universities have now introduced Business ethics as a compulsory subject for the postgraduate students and professional courses.

The book has been divided into six sections and in total 16 chapters–

Part–I Ethics–An introduction

Part –II Ethics in organization

Part –III Ethical choices in business

Part –IV Corporate social responsibilities

Part –V Ethics in different management practices

Part –VI Business and society

In spite of the fact that a good number of literatures is available in the market, I do feel this book would provide fundamental concepts about business ethics to not only management students but also managers, corporate leaders, decision makers etc.

There are many who have helped and inspired me–colleagues, friends, and all my family members, close relatives. I also thank the whole team of New Age international Ltd., New Delhi, Publishing house who took keen interest at every step in publishing this book.

Constructive suggestions for the qualitative improvement cf the book will be highly appreciated. I will be rewarded if the book meets the need of those for whom it is meant.

Author

Content

Part V – Ethics in Different Management Practice

Part VI – Business and Society

Part I

Ethics–An Introduction

Chapter 1

Introduction–Ethics and Business Ethics

- *Introduction*
- *Meaning and Definition of Ethics*
- *Nature and Objective of Ethics*
- *Ethics and Related Terms*
- *Meaning of Business Ethics*
- *Need and Objective of Business Ethics*
- *Significance of Business Ethics*
- *Summary*
- *Case Study*

1.1 AN INTRODUCTION TO ETHICS

Ethics is not a recent discovery. Over the centuries philosophers in their struggle with human behavior have developed different approaches to ethics, each leading to different conclusion.

The word "Ethics" which is coined from the Latin word 'Ethics' and Greek word 'Ethikos' pertains to character. Ethics is thus said to be the science of conduct. As a matter of fact it deals with certain standard of human conduct and morals.

The field of ethics involves systematizing, defending and recommending concepts of right and wrong behavior. Ethics is a mass of moral principles or set of values about what is right or wrong, true or false, fair or unfair, proper or improper what is right is ethical and what is wrong is unethical.

1.2 MEANING AND DEFINITION OF ETHICS

Peter F. Drucker writes— "There is only one ethics, one set of rules of morality, one code that of individual behavior in which the same rules apply to everyone alike."

Philip Wheel Wright says— "Ethics is the branch of philosophy which is the systematic study of selective choice, of the standards of right and wrong and by which it may ultimately be directed.

Swami Vivekananda has set the tone for ethics. He says- "Supreme oneness is the rationale of all ethics and morality. Ethics cannot be derived from the mere sanction to any personage. Some eternal principle of truth has the sanction of ethics. Where is the eternal sanction to be found except in the only infinite reality that exists in you and us and in all, in the self, in the soul?"

Discussion on ethics cannot be completed without Swami's views on ethics. He suggested ethics as the degree of faith in oneself.

Ethics comes from the attainment of freedom, renunciation, which comes only when the individual attain a superior strength.

According to Swamiji— " The difference between weakness and strength is of a heaven degree; the difference between virtue and vice is that of a degree; the difference between and hell is that of a degree, all differences in this world are of degrees and not a kind of characteristics."

"An individual is an infinite circle whose center is every where and circumference no where ethics disappears in the situations where people recon to the thinking," I am pure, others are impure.

So in short, we can say that ethics goes beyond the immediate facts that pertain to a moral question— What the situation is, it addresses the question of what ought to be?

The inner content of individual, the character of individual can lead ethical individuality to ethical collectivity.

The ethical, the right thing to do, is action that best serves the ideas of honesty, integrity, morality and good management practices.

1.3 NATURE AND OBJECTIVES OF ETHICS

The liberalization and globalization being sweep changes in the concept of doing business, but the major by-product like corruption, favoritism and nepotism, deterioration of human values, series of scam in business, govt. policies and society are also produced in the 21st century.

There is a loss of faith in instruments of society. Business houses are becoming big with control of large resources, human, financial and technical but their surviving purposes to society are always having the doubtful values. Day by day innocent Indians are losing their faith in laws, courts and govt.

At one side business enterprise are coping up with intense emerged competition and on the other side they are violating the principles of proper public conduct.

In the wake of mounting scandals corporations, all around the world are adopting ethical conduct, code of ethics. They are excellent organizations, which have shown a spurt of activity towards evaluation of goals, concepts, values management and conduct.

Ethical issues are more critical today than they have ever been. Similarly the increased interest with ethics in India is also related to many issues as nexus between business, crime, politics, a series of scams , sordid events of the past few years in the public affairs of the country which have led many in the country to believe that the country is approaching destruction unless it reforms ethics.

In terms of practically applied the terms ethics and values became an important concern in the U.S. in the eighties.

But fortunately the application of ethics in theory and practice in new millennium is gaining momentum rapidly. As the all India council foe technical education which regulates the management education in India has in December 1995, recommended the inclusion of business ethics as a course in management studies curriculum.

Objectives of Ethics

The objectives of ethics are as below:

1. The very basic objective is to define the greatest good of man and establish a standard for the same.
2. Set/Establish moral standards/norms of behavior.
3. An overall study of human behavior: what is moral or immoral should be assessed.
4. Apply judgement upon human behavior based on these standard and norms.
5. Suggest moral behavior, Prescribes recommendations about Do's and Don'ts.
6. One's opinion or attitude about human conduct is expressed in general.

Nature of Ethics

The nature of ethics can be explained by these points:

1. The concept of ethics is applied to human beings only as they have freedom of choice and means of free will. They can only decide the degree of ends they wish to pursue and the means to achieve the ends.
2. The study of ethics is nothing but a field of social science in which a set of systematic knowledge about moral behavior and human conduct is learned.
3. Ethics deals with human conduct which is voluntary not forced by circumstances or humans. So we can say that at the ground level ethics deals with moral judgement regarding set directed human conduct.
4. The science of ethics is a normative science. It is a search for an ideal litmus test of proper behavior. Normative science involves arriving at moral standards that regulate right and wrong conduct.

1.4 ETHICS AND RELATED TERMS

To understand ethics thoroughly, we need to see its relevance with some quite similar terms:

(A) *Ethics and Morality*: a morality is a set of rules to guide the actions of an individual human-being. Rand says about it –"a code of value to guide man's choice and actions." So ethics and morality would seem to be synonymous but exactly it is not so.

As morality refers to the rules and guidelines which an individual or a group has about what is right/wrong, good or evil same as ethical principles also give an idea about right or wrong, true or false.

Really speaking, to differentiate between ethics and morality is a difficult task as human behavior is influenced by emotions and sentiments. As many big organizations and big businessmen have no predetermined ethics but they may evaluate the good conduct of business on the basis of customs, expectations of society, some beliefs. But in way ethics is not merely the code of conduct based on customs, conventions and the accepted courtesies of a society but it is the code of conduct developed by proper testing to guide the human behavior. In short, Ethics and morality, for all purpose may be assumed to mean the same.

(B) *Ethics and Religion*: Though ethics is not synonymous to religion morality is a primary force in shaping our ethics.

Thomas M. Garrett writes— "The religion derive their moral percepts not only from human experience but from divine revelation. It must rely on the unaided human reason."

Ethics gets idea from religion and thorough experiments it approves them as- "code of conduct." The development of ethics is dependent on the religious morality. The great historian Arnold J. Toynbee writes—"No society could succeed without any religious aim. Mere desire for prosperity cannot motivate a person for building up an enduring dynamic and progressive nation."

Needless to say, about the vital role of ethics in our economic life which could be activated on the basis of religious principle?

(C) *Ethics and Law*: Hosmer (1995) says – Respect for law as an ethical value– What is law? Law is a code of conduct which the authority in power prescribes for society. It is concerned with the minimum regulation necessary for public order which is enacted by govt. So Govt. gives shape to only those minimum social obligations, customs or traditions which are essential to be complied with by the people.

It basically differs from ethics in its option to use force when necessary and in fact it is backed by power.

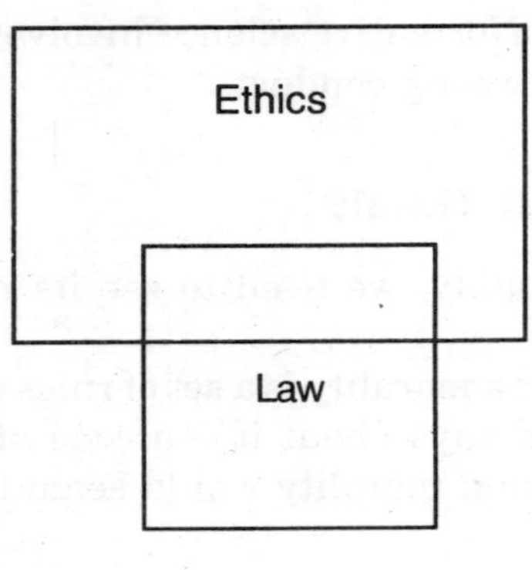

The most important divergence between ethics and law is that ethics concentrate on the do's and laws on the don'ts. Ethics is a much wider term than law.

The required ethical behavior may not be covered by the law at all. 'look after the aged', 'be considerate to your workers', 'Teach well to your students', 'Do not tell a lie', Obey your elders',— will fall within the circle of ethics but not within that of law.

(D) *Ethics and Values*: Moral values are deep-seated ideas and feelings that manifest themselves as behavior or conduct. These values are not so easy to measure or express in words.

There is very thin line which distinguishes between ethics and values both drive what is right and what is wrong in human conduct and what 'ought to be'. But then also a relationship can be derived between value and ethics like this

Law + Knowledge = Ethics

So as, we know the consequences of our actions, we can convert values into rules of behavior that can be derived as ethics.

1.5 INTRODUCTION TO BUSINESS ETHICS

In any organization from top executive to bottom line employees, ethics is considered as everybody business. It is not just only achieving high level of economic performance but also to conduct one of business's most important social challenges, ethically at the same time. Here what we get a combination of two familiar words—'Ethics and Business' in 'Business Ethics'. Different meaning is given to business as follows:

- Business ethics are the application of general ethical rules to business behavior.
- Business ethics are rules of business by which propriety of business activity may be judged.

By Cater Mcnamara— "Business ethics is generally coming to know what is right or wrong in the workplace and doing what is right—this is in regard to effects of products/ services and in relationship with stake holders".

"Attention to ethics in workplace sensitizes managers and staff to know they should act so that they retain a strong moral compass. Consequently, business ethics can be strong preventive medicine."

According to John Donaldson- Business ethics in short can be desired as the systematic study of ethical matters pertaining to business industry or related activities, institutions and beliefs. Business ethics is the systematic handling of values in business and industry.

- Business ethics are the rules of business by which the propriety of business activity may be judged.
- Business ethics concentrate on moral standard as they apply to business policies, institutions and behavior. It is a specialized study of moral right or wrong. It is a form of applied ethics.

- Business ethics are nothing but the application of ethics in business. It proves that business can be and have been ethical and still make profits. Today more and more interest is being given to the application of ethical practices in business dealings and the ethical implications of business.

The 3 C's of Business ethics:

1. Compliance: (The need for compliance of rules including):
   - Laws
   - principles of morality
   - policy of the company
2. The Contribution (Business can make to the society):
   - The core values
   - Quality of products/services
   - Employment
   - Usefulness of activities to surrounding activities
   - QWL
3. The Consequences of business activity:
   - Toward environment inside and outside the organization
   - Social responsibility toward shareholders, bankers, customers and employees of organization.
   - Good public image, sound activity- good image.

1.6 NEED AND OBJECTIVES OF BUSINESS ETHICS

Need of business ethics:

1. Business operates within the society.
2. Every business irrespective of size exists more on ethical means or in total regards to all its social concern to survive long.
3. Business needs to function as responsible corporate citizen in the country.

Objectives of Business Ethics

According to Peter Pratley–Business ethics has a two fold objectives-'it evaluates human practices by calling upon moral standards, also it may give prescription advice on how to act morally in a specific kind of situation'.

(A) Analysis and Evaluation

Ethical analysis and ethical diagnosis of past events, happenings, clarifying the standards, uncover the moral values, habits of thought.

How to evaluate the situation? Ethics provides rational methods for answering the present situation and related future issues. A well equipped information is a must to achieve this second objective, a careful assessment of relevant information will lead to balanced judgments.

(B) Approaches to Resolve Ethical Dilemmas

It provides therapeutic advice when facing the present dilemmas and future dangers. Only the condition which requires a true identification of relevant stakeholder and a clear-cut understanding of crucial issues at stake.

1.7 SIGNIFICANCE OF BUSINESS ETHICS

"Good business ethics promotes good business"

This statement is supported by the research findings of some well known authorities– Raymond Baumhart, Brener and Molander, and Strom and Ruch. It was clear from their findings that only those businesses can develop on a long term bases which conducts activities on ethical grounds.

Once 'Robert Day' has said that good ethics not only promotes professionalism in management but it purify the inner mind of every business man.

Another writer Thomas Donaldson (Ethics in business- a new look) has observed that-"there are some key reasons why business ethics is vital and why ethics plays a key role in business."

(1) Positive Consequences

Business depends on the approval of the society, acceptance of rules, mutual trusts and confidence. Prof. Robert Day writes—"when ethical conduct is displayed, it puts some kind of trust and confidence in relationship." So business with ethics always leads to positive consequences.

(2) Goodwill of the Business and Businessman

Good ethical behavior will increase the goodwill of both business as well as the businessman. Strong public image is a symptom of success in the long run. On the other hand, once an organization's image is tarnished it would have direct consequences on sales, profits, morale or day-to-day running of the business.

(3) Protection—Both Sides

If ethical implications are there in organization businessmen act more sincerely and the level of commitment would be higher. Ethics protects people in dealing with each other. Prof. Robert Day writes "Good ethics is sound business insurance."

(4) Self-satisfaction

In the dynamic world, businessmen are seeking self satisfaction, mental relief, free from anxiety, release tension. To attain the inner satisfaction certain people consider only good ethics can promote good business.

As a businessman is first a member of the society than a businessman, so some do not implement a decision which stands on unethical ground because it wouldn't provide the satisfaction to their sub-conscious mind.

(5) Encourage Others

When a few people start following ethics side by side to profit making, they encourage, motivate others and set examples for them. As Prof. Learned and Associates writes—"Businessman who follows the ethical principles in the conduct of business, motivates others also, to follow the same principles."

(6) Success and Development

Ethical conduct of business leads to development and series of success. Learned writes—'A sincere person who does hard work becomes ethical and always succeed in his efforts but an unethical person cannot'.

(7) New Management

In the era of global economy, new principles are required in new management. Prof. 'Day' writes that management cannot become a profession so far as it does not follow good ethics. An important feature of a profession is that it has a laid down code of conduct which remains on all the principles of "service to humanity.

So to run the good business in modern scenario you have to develop and follow ethics.

SUMMARY

This chapter defines ethics as some standardized form of conduct or a mass of moral principles about what conduct ought to be.

To understand ethics it is necessary to study the relation of ethics with some similar terms like èthics and morality, ethics and law, ethics and value and ethics and religion.

Ethics in business and management is gaining momentum day by day. Business ethics are the application of general ethical rules to business behavior. The significance of business ethics in 21st century scenario is remarkable; this chapter throws light on some practical ethical principles which can be directly followed by companies.

QUESTIONS

1. Elaborate the term ethics.
2. Explain in detail the meaning, nature and objective of ethics.
3. What is business ethics? What are the needs for business ethics?
4. "Good business ethics promotes good business". Explain the significance of business ethics in 21st century scenario.

CASE STUDY - 1

Sanjay Verma was an MBA; He had specialized in Marketing and Advertising. He has just joined XYZ Ad Agency, though a competent and innovative person with outstanding performance during his stay at the MBA institute, yet he got this job with great difficulty due to recession in the jòb market. He had somehow managed to find this job through a contact of his uncle. The chairman of the company wanted him to somehow persuade a well known newspaper to avoid reporting on a controversial corruption charge against him and instead write a favorable editorial. Raman was not convinced that his chairman was clean in the case; on the other hand, the newspaper was willing to accommodate the chairman, if the organization came out with a large size advertisement in his favor.

Recently, Sanjay's father died leaving his wife and three sisters on the verge of marriage with Sanjay alone in a disastrous condition to help himself and his family.

What should Sanjay do?

CASE STUDY - 2

Amit was a young and dynamic manager at ABC Private Ltd. and was recently married.

Due to nature of his job, he had to do lot of traveling and therefore unable to devote his time for his wife. At one time he was away for 25 days tour only to return for a day and again go for 10 days tour. This situation led to differences in his married life, turning to serious note. Once he took his wife along with him to tour and found that he and his wife could stay in hotel within permissible limits of his lodging and boarding allowance with no extra burden on his company. Thus he was away for work for a good part of the day but could spend time with his wife in the evening. This situation worked out perfectly for himself and his wife and their relations became very good. Therefore he started taking his wife along with him on his tours.

Is it ethical on part of Amit?

Chapter 2

The Concepts of New Ethics

- *Introduction*
- *Ethical Dimensions*
- *Factors Causing Unethical Behavior*
- *Important Factors of Building an Ethical Infrastructure*
- *Summary*
- *Case Study*

2.1 INTRODUCTION

The new economy has brought greater transparency and greater flexibility but also greater complexity and therefore new and greater risks. It has become very crucial to look at how the new economy had brought greater complexity to the business environment changing the ethical dimension and raising new ethical issues.

It goes on to outline the varied dimension of the new economy like—Globalization, technology, assets, framework, recruiting and retaining the talent.

These factors have brought so many changes and challenges to the company policies regards to their management practices, relationships in different domestic, international, multinational and global contents. So to establish an ethical infrastructure and integrate ethics in organization working we need to study the ethics in new economy keeping the consideration of those mentioned dimensions.

2.2 ETHICAL DIMENSIONS

1. Globalization

The growing integration of economies and societies around the world has been one of the most hotly debated topics in international economies over the past few years. Many forces are driving globalization—Communication, improved infrastructure, technology, regulation, free trade and free movement of people. Rapid growth and poverty reduction in India, China and other countries that were poor 20 years ago, has been positive aspect of globalization. On the other hand, globalization has also generated significant international opposition over concerns that it has increased inequality and environmental degradation.

Ethics, morality and globalization are connected with each other the ethical dimension of globalization is beginning to be debated world widely.

The renowned utilitarian philosopher Peter Singer puts the questions attached to globalization in this way—"To what extent should leaders see their role narrowly, in terms of promoting the interests of their citizens every where"?

D.Wheeler and M. Sillanpaa, in the stakeholder corporation a blue print for maximizing shareholders value, calculate that 200 corporations in the world have sales equivalent to one-third of the world's total economic activity.

So at a business level, we talk of globalization when companies decide to take part in the emerging global economy and establish themselves in foreign markets.

To meet the objectives first they adapt their products and services to the final user's linguistic and cultural requirement, which is not all an easy task manager have to manage the workforce in different languages, different cultures, and different tax procedures.

The basic need in the globalization era is to control the ethical conflicts to its minimum level though its not so easy to achieve. Though some ways can be suggested like—

- Sensitive and sympathetic attitudes towards local customs.
- Awareness about world pressure group.
- Know and comply with local laws related to tax, employment and finance.
- Manage diversity within and across the national boundaries.

2. Technology

Technology is a driving force helping business organization to face the challenges of today's competitive business environment. It is revolutionizing the nature and speed of communication within and between companies.

All the functional areas of organization—Marketing, finance, HR, production etc. are being facilitated by it.

The global development of companies is very much affected by technology. Technology has been catalyst for this development.

Though there are some social and ethical issues related to technology:

(*a*) Complexity and integrity

(*b*) Software piracy

(*c*) Monitoring
(*d*) Harassment
(*e*) Employment
(*f*) Privacy
(*g*) Accessibility

These are some yardsticks, following which the managers can tackle some ethical risks attached to technology—

- Take care of the flow of information about data in and out of the organization.
- The monitoring of the use of e-mail and uses of internet in an effective way
- Participative management development as to discuss the practicalities and get the feedback.

3. Intangible Assets

"Everything that can be counted does not necessarily count; everything that counts cannot necessarily be counted." [Albert Einstein (1879–1955), American theoretical physicist]

The most valuable assets as far as an organization context in the new economy are called as in tangible assets. Intangible assets are non-scarce; these increase in values when used as they are not subject to diminishing returns as the tangible assets, but have increasing returns.

As all intangibles (customer, employee, leadership, culture, strategy, brand, innovation, knowledge, intellectual property rights) are future oriented so they create future value.

The ethical points of discussions related to intangible assets are a lot like—

(*a*) Intangibles are difficult to manage and exclusively control
(*b*) Intangibles investments are typically more risky
(*c*) Intangibles cannot be directly measured and their value

4. The War for Talent

In 1997, a Land Mark Mckinsey and Company study exposed the "War for talent" as a strategic business challenge and a critical driver of corporate performance. In the new book "the war for talent" the authors of the original study reveal that hot economic times and cool talent management is critical to every company's success.

As talented, skilled, knowledgeable people with innovative ideas are among the most valuable assets (intangible of the 21st century so they are becoming more valuable than ever. Recruitment, selection as well as retaining talented people is a big challenge before the organization.

By providing attractive financial incentives companies are behind to recruit and retain talent, but these are not so sufficient, for this the 95 theses of the cluetrain manifesto provide some creative insight into what are the leading forces which motivate employees to be in an organization. "Notably, they want their companies to learn to speak to them in a new way, honestly and humanely. If the companies do not learn to do this (thesis 89) employee will vote with their feet."

Companies who do a better job of addressing the needs of the Genx'ers will find themselves in a best position.

The Cluetrain manifesto explained the category of generation "X" after Douglas Coupland's book of that title. They are highly talented, skilled with a valuable ethical value system, set of attitudes, self confident, immediate authority.

Their relationship with their employer must be mutual friendly and win-win type.

These people will remain in the type of organization where they find a true alignment between their own value system and organization's value and beliefs.

However, companies who do not have recruitment and retaining strategy will soon find themselves spending much more money to attract the best talent.

Studies show that the companies that are most responsive to employees need have lower turnover in staff.

'Fortune magazine' publishes a list of the 100 best companies to work for in the U.S., based on the research conducted by Hewitt, a human-resources consultancy. Where skills shortages are most acute, companies are most responsive to their people's need, 42% of the top 100 are IT or financial services firm.

So in short we say that in the war for talent if you really want to retain and hold talent in your organization, it is essential to follow some practical steps—

- Discover the needs, wants of talented people behind joining a firm or being there.
- Calculate the total package which must include the total tangibles elements and just compare it against the competitors.
- Assessment of the gaps which come out from the expectations of employees and the realities.
- Find out the reasons, why people leave the organization and try to avoid the same reasons for the future, learn from them.
- Try to generate a healthy balance between employee's work and their other portion of life.

Simply telling people or merely teaching managers about ethics will not encourage ethical conduct in the organization, some extra efforts are needed. In fact the basic and foremost important is to develop commitment to ethics.

- Commitment to ethics is the most valuable asset the firms can posses. Which is very difficult to acquire and maintain?
- It might be possible that it is somewhere in the company but not at all levels or not anywhere to be effective.
- In these situation unethical practices in business arise, which show the failure of the business firms to pay attention to ethical risks that are created by their own systems, policies and practices.

'Walton' writes—that business ethics is related with truth and justice and has various components like expectations of society healthy competition, consumer freedom and good behavior. All people expect that each and every conduct and activity should have a strong foundation of ethics but in practice, it finds that a strong foundation of ethics but in practice, it finds that business is involved in unethical practices.

2.3 FACTORS CAUSING UNETHICAL BEHAVIOR

1. Competition—'Litemer and Molander' have found in their studies in 1974 that the important cause of decreasing use of ethical conduct in business is the increasing nature of competition. When managers try to meet goals and have to cut corners at that moment this acute competition at national as well as international level becomes an unavoidable reason foe unethical conduct.
2. There is an increasing pressure to earn more profit and to cope with the enlarged requirements and expectations of all like shareholders, customers, employees or all the categories of its stakeholders. So this becomes an important factor of unethical conduct of business.
3. Ambiguous Situations create the ethical dilemma to the manager and selection of an alternative which gives them higher return at the cost of losing integrity they don't think.
4. Political corruption has also become a big issue now-a-days; As business cannot be aloof from politics and most of the political parties demand gifts, donations and bribes from the business men for their political gain.
5. Social values and customs are not followed by new generation.
6. Now-a-days people want to become rich in a short while even by doing unethical acts. Money and success becomes the important motivator behind any activity.
7. People neglect the social responsibility, lack of integrity and discipline in the social values

Many of the business activities which involve unethical activities are objectionable, exploitative and create big problems to innocent people. A sample of these unethical conducts is shown below:

- Encourage practices of corruption
- False representation of returns and income statements
- Ignore the social interest
- Creation of acute competition
- Political donations
- Exploit the consumer
- Illegal trade with enemy countries
- Exploit scare natural resources.

The points mentioned above are some real practical situations which are embedded in business organization and are sometimes unavoidable and therefore corporate commitment to ethics is vital, it is a most valuable asset a firm can possess, which pays in long run. A few of practical examples of the corporate world, where the commitment level of ethics is very high.

(*a*) Johnson and Johnson—an ethical commitment to health and safety of consumers is deep-rooted in J & J. many persons died after consuming Tylenol capsules contaminated with poison. As it deals with sensitive area and protection to public is a must so the managers took over all capsules from all the places world-wide.

This crisis incident worked as a catalyst that boosted J & J's image in eye of customer world-wide.

(*b*) JBM provides ethical treatment of employees so they get the loyalty from employees, thefts, cheating and frauds are nowhere seen over there.

"Ethical behavior isn't an act but a habit, just as good health requires cultivating the habits of getting enough sleep and eating wholesome food, Aristotle believed that right action was the result of developing good moral habits. In a business context, this means training and at the deepest level, something we call, corporate culture".

—*Jim Kelly, Chairman and CEO of United Parcel Post Service*

2.4 IMPORTANT FACTORS OF BUILDING AN ETHICAL INFRASTRUCTURE

Some important factors of building an ethical infrastructure in the organization are as follows:

1. Commitment from Top Management

As the top executives are the leaders, so if an ethical initiation is taken by them, it would be easy to spread it downside.

Ethical behavior should be fully supported by the top management. They must set some examples in front of the employees from their own level if commitment to ethics.

Ethics committee: Some boards have established a separate ethics committee which oversee development and operation of ethics program.

Some companies do have full time ethics officer, like USAA, a diversified financial service company. The chief executive officer, Robert T. Herres, is the chief ethics officer and he appoints an ethics coordinator to oversee the program.

This committee may consist of internal and external directors. According to Koontz and Weihrich, this committee will perform the following functions:

1. Holding regular meetings to discuss ethical issues.
2. Dealing with grey areas.
3. Communicating the codes to all members of the organization.
4. Checking of the possible violations of the code.
5. Enforcing the codes.
6. Rewarding compliance and punishing violation.
7. Reporting activities of the committee to the board of directors.

2. Code of Ethics

To establish and to encourage ethical conduct formal codes of ethics for organization members must be framed. These corporate codes of ethics vary in quality and substance. Some of these consist of a set of specific rules, a list of do's and don'ts.

A code of ethics states an organization's basic and primary values and the ethical rules, so the rules of conduct are like a general value statement which lacks a framework of meaning and purpose.

Code of conduct are not merely rules and regulations, their scope is somewhat different! A code cannot list and mandate every form of ethical and unethical conduct. A good corporate code of values and conduct should include certain managerial and employee guidelines for making ethical decisions.

'Frank Doly' of Northrop Grumman has suggested—"Codes of conduct should be policies that are easy to read, who don't like to read can't read, easily understood by people or respond much better to visual information." Take creative license in the presentation.

Some organization have reduced voluminous codes of conduct to just a few core values, for Example, Texan Instruments a global semiconductor company, ended up their codes of conduct with just 3 words–Integrity, Innovation and Commitment.

A list of code of ethics is given below:

- Do not use abusive language
- Manage personal finance well
- Demonstrate courtesy, respect, honesty, fairness
- Exhibit good attendance
- Conduct business in compliance with law
- Follow all accounting rules and control
- True claims in product advertisements.

3. Communicating Ethics

The best ethics program in the world is the one which is communicated well. The communication should be in various forms and frequently occur. Communicating of all code of ethics, core values can be done by an easy way—written form supplemented with some questions in the form of feedback. The supervisors can hold meeting with employees to discuss ethical concerns.

A proper well designed communication network is needed to institutionalizing ethics. Therefore, Purcell and James Weber suggest that this can be accomplished in 3 ways–

- By establishing appropriate company policy and ethical rules
- By using a formally appointed ethics committee
- By teaching ethics in management development program.

4. Ethics Training

There is a great need for ethics training because only communicating well is not sufficient to convert values into practice, sometimes employee may think that they know each and every aspect about ethics, ethical decision making but they might be unaware of the ideas of the actual evaluation process, implementation and consequences of the decision making. Therefore ethical training program are very crucial. Effective ethics training should have–

- Employee participation to exchange views with each other open discussion of realistic ethical issues.
- Clarify the ethical values and enhance the ethical awareness of employees.
- Define criteria for ethical decision making within the organization.
- Being detailed, extensive to accomplish anything significant.

- A clear intense focus on ethical issue of the organization.
- Investigate ethical environment, analysis the activities, strategies, resources, policies and goals and after examining go on enriching them.

5. Ethics Officer

An ethics specialist is a full-fledged member of the board of director. He has a "kitchen cabinet" to serve as a sounding board and to drive ownership of the program throughout all areas of business. He acts as a guide for ethical conduct and ethical decision making. The ethics officer provides some resources for assistance to the employees of the organization, so that if they find any wrong doings while working, they can report directly to him.

For e.g. at USAA, the ethics coordinator is part of the CEO's office and works closely with the company's ethical council, a group of senior executive who review issues of major significance and take appropriate actions.

6. Response and Enforcement

Implementing an ethical program consistently is one of the biggest challenges for organizations. A consistent response to ethical issues involves so many criteria like– Reward system (for them who have shown ethical character), built in incentives, this can be further supported by checklist method.

According to Bennett, employee can be taught to apply the following checklist when confronted with an ethical dilemma:

1. Identifying the dilemma
2. Collect the facts
3. Make a list of your options
4. Test each options
5. Make your decision.

A consistent enforcement by carefully coordinating with human resources personnel or by establishing an ethics coordinating committee that can review or hear appeals on disciplinary actions.

7. Audits, Revisions and Refinements

Audits should establish to reveal whether communication about ethical codes of conduct works well or not? What are the results of training program? A detailed investigation about potential violations of law or regulation. The experts in audit committee would be executives of the organization or can be hired from outside consultants. Many companies are finding effective ways to judge about the effectiveness of their program like surveys, focus groups and detailed exit interviews often conducted by outside consultants for unbiased feedback. A review for value program must be allowed. In this dynamic world, every month, every year circumstances change which demand managers to reevaluate the goals and content of their program, sometimes after the evaluation, managers find to begin with a fresh look as well as a courageous hand to stop the continuation of an idea whose time has passed.

SUMMARY

The new economy has brought greater complexity to the business environment, changing the ethical dimension and raising new ethical issue some driving factors like technological changes, intangible assets, effects of globalization, the war for talent are the important ones. Recognizing unethical conduct and remove it from the root has become an important need. Although ethical management is being given a higher priority by management team, a wealth of evidence reveals that managers are still unclear about how to go on strategic thinking and cultural building that encourage ethical conduct in the organization.

QUESTIONS

1. Discuss about varied dimensions of new economy.
2. Explain in detail the factors causing un-ethical behavior in organizations.
3. Write an essay about building ethical infrastructure in an organization.

CASE STUDY – 1

Mrs. Rekha Mittal is a Vice President and head of strategic planning division, of Indian based multinational firm. She long believed in slogan "When in Rome do as Roman's do", but in recent years she has been forced to rethink that position. In 1990, when the company considered opening a manufacturing branch in South Africa, it finally decided against the move, because of the then existing apartheid laws which mandated racial segregation and discrimination against black. She is now faced with three some what similar situations or were they similar? First, the company has the opportunity to contract at an excellent price for fabric woven in China. However she has reports that the fabric probably came from factories employing forced labor. A second opportunity is to buy clothing manufactured in Pakistan. Again, however she has reports that her sources are using child labor, usually girls under 14 yrs. of age. Her third opportunity is to open a plant in Saudi Arabia. In this situation she is warned that for the operation to be successful, women should not be placed in executive positions because they would not be taken seriously by those with they had to deal.

CASE STUDY – 2

An Airplane manufacturer has spent great deal of money developing a new airplane. The company badly needs cash because it is financially over extended. If it does not get some large orders soon, it will have to close down some part of its operation. Doing that will put several thousand workers out of job. The result will be disastrous not only for the workers but also for the town in which they live. The President of the company has been trying to interest the government of a foreign country in a large purchase. He learns that one of the key governmental ministers in charge of making final decision is heavily in debt because of gambling. He quietly contacts that minister and offers him 10 Lakh in cash if he awards the contracts for five planes to his firm. The money is paid and the contract is awarded.

Chapter 3

Values and Ethics

3.1 INTRODUCTION

Is capital punishment right or wrong? How about the racial quotas in hiring are they just or unjust? The answers to these questions are value laden. For example, some might indulge in the argument that capital punishment is right because it is an appropriate retribution for crimes such as murder. However, on the other hand, others might argue, that no govt. has the right to take anyone's life.

Value — What we choose as worth while or believe to have merit, in a general or broad sense. Issues of right or wrong are related to one's 'values' Values are our standard of right and wrong. Whether something is right or wrong is not a matter of fact. It is a matter of opinion. An action may be upheld by some one as very right while others might have contrary view. So values represent:

- "a specific mode of conduct or end state of existence is personally or socially preferable to an opposite or converse mode of conduct or end-state of existence."

  – *'Stephen P. Robbins'*

> *'Edward Spranger'* defines the values—"as the constellation of likes, dislikes, viewpoints, inner inclinations, rational and irrational judgments, prejudices, and association pattern that determine a person's view of the world."

Values are the deep–seated ideas and feelings that manifest themselves as behavior or conduct these values. The true reflection of one's values is his/her action.

3.2 CHARACTERISTICS OF VALUES

1. Values tend to be relatively stable and enduring. A significant portion of the values, we hold is established in our early years from parents, teachers and others. So these values are originally learned.
2. Values constitute the foundations of one's character. They are at the core of personality and a powerful force affecting behavior.
3. Values are abstract representation of what people believe to be right, proper and worth while to pursue.
4. Some values are not fixed, but they change our time and situation.
5. Values have intensity and content attributes in which the content attribute says that a mode of conduct or end-state of existence is important and the intensity attribute explains how important it is.
6. The values which are internalized by an individual, becomes a part of his personality, then they go beyond the zone of choice for the person concerned. His action based on these values then become spontaneous and continuous, automotive and instinctive.

3.3 VALUE FORMATION IN SOCIETY

When we rank an individual's values in terms of their intensity, we obtain that person's value system. All of us have a hierarchy of values that forms our value system. This system is identified by the relative importance we assign to such values as: freedom, self respect, pleasure honesty, obedience and equality.

For a particular person to accept a particular value into his value system he must first find out the worth of the pursuits of his life. The values in an individual's value system are introduced and later reinforced over a life time of experience, but more particularly during growing up, formative years of individual.

During this period various social institutions play important role in inculcating values in the individuals value system, the major are:

(*a*) The family one is born into.

(*b*) The school and other educational institutions and all extra-curriculum bodies—games and clubs.

(*c*) One's religion.

(*d*) The society or community one belongs to.

So the values fostered by each of these institutions reinforce the values taught by others and together they form the value system of an individual.

Individual value formation is best understood in the frame work of social psychology theories.

'***Secord and Backman***'—described two approaches:

(*a*) Intra-individual Approaches

Focus on the function of variables within the individual. Psychologists have traditionally limited themselves to the individual, engaging in a quest for 'genotypic' traits which provides the basis for predicting the subject's behavior with many kinds of people in many situations. In this approach, behavioral social patterns reflect the intra-individual structures or mechanism such as habits, needs cognitive structures or most frequently personality straits.

(*b*) Inter-individual Approaches

It focuses on the function of external variables: "a person's behavior is mostly a reflection of the situation he happens to be in. Inherent in the situation is the social forces that shape and determine his behavior at any movement, although it is recognized that his previous experiences with such situations have predisposed him to react in certain ways in particular circumstances".

Because of inherent limitations of both approaches a combination explanation for behaviour seems likely and has been called the interpersonal approach.

An Individual's actions are affected by societal values as well as genetic and internal factors. An Individual learns societal norms, values and customs through direct or vicarious experiences and these values are enforced by society through group pressure. There is usually a range of acceptable behaviors and the individual choose behaviour within this range.

In short, in developing a value system an individual is influenced by both the external environment and the internal cognitive structure. This value system is affected by the culture and subcultures to which an individual belongs.

3.4 TYPES OF VALUES

According to M. Rokeach, (The nature of Human values, New York; free poses 1973) there are two types of values:

(*i*) *Instrument values*:

The values which concern the way we approach the end states. These relate to means for achieving desired result.

Some are like:

- Hard work and achievement
- Education and intellectual pursuits
- Self sufficiency; independence
- Truthfulness; honesty

- Assertiveness; Standing up for yourself
- Being well mannered and courteous towards others
- Open-mindedness; receptivity to new ideas.
- Caring towards others.

(*ii*) *Terminal values*:

They are those end state goals that we praise such as comfortable life, a sense of accomplishment, equality among all people:

- Happiness; satisfaction in life
- Peace and harmony in the world
- Knowledge and wisdom
- Pride in accomplishment
- Security; freedom from threat.

3.5 ETHICAL VALUE SYSTEM

Everything that we see, here, say, imagine or do can be divided into two main categories:

(*a*) The way situations are

(*b*) The way situations ought to be.

How situations ought to be is what gives rise to 'values'. These values are not so easy to measure or express in words. In this regard, Chakraborty (1991, 1993 and 1995) has made useful efforts to establish relationship between values and ethics. He says: "As the consciousness in the individual–in his/her equation with nature, with the infinite, with the Adorable energy, with Brahmand-begins to ascend holistic heights, a major outcome becomes evident in the share of his/her relationship with others".

If we know the consequences of our action, we can convert values into rules of behavior that can be described as ethics

Value + Knowledge = Ethics

Any initiation of an action begins with an inventory of values. These get converted to intentions for action, which then get articulated as actual behavior. All these behavior results in consequences to oneself as well as to others. They either damage or enhance the values of the affected person.

Value leads to–Intention leads to–Behavior leads to–Consequences.

One of the important lessons to learn in ethics is to see life as it is, without our perceptions and attitudes distorting it to fit in with what we want to see it. All of us react, not to reality it self, but to our own interpretation of reality. Our behavior is affected not by particular situation but how we see and what we see in that situation. When we describe the world around us or people in it, we in effect describe ourselves, our perception, attitudes, our morality and our ethical value system.

"***Stephen R. Covey***" — " The seven habits of highly effective people– tates that the individual value system rises out of 'inside-out' approach. Inside-out means to start with self even more fundamentally to start with the most inside part of self–with one's paradigms, one's characters and one's motives." For example, if one wants to be trusted by others then he has to be first trust worthy, there is no other technique, facts or strategy to get others to trust you if you are not trust worthy. Covey says in his inside out approach that "private victories precede public victories—that keeping and making promises to ourselves precede keeping promises to others."

3.6 ETHICS AND VALUE MAXIMIZATION

When ethics and values are taken together, we should do the analysis of ethics in relation to value maximization to find out the value of ethics for people working in any organization.

First, of all we'll find how ethical behavior and value maximization are related with each other. As we know there are no universal standards as to what constitutes ethical behavior, which means that a broad array of value maximizing corporate policies might violate individual notion of ethical behavior.

Does value maximization in an organization simply means as short cut profit maximization? No! A very deep understanding of ethical standards are required for value maximization, a typical economic discussion of short run profit maximization is not at all sufficient.

Ethical and Trust

Trust is one of the most important ethical complements, they are compatible with each other as ethical behavior leads to trust.

If we start from a very basic transaction between individuals, any transaction involves a promise to deliver a particular good/service, in so and so condition in exchange for a promised payment by the other party. So if any kind of mistrust or corruption takes place in any of the transaction and justice of the economic system will be harshly impaired. And the impact of corruption will be negative to efficiency.

So we find that trust and trust worthiness are very essential to economic efficiency, without it, it is not possible to support long term debt or the instruments that accompany it. So we find that Ethical behaviour is highly responsible for building trust among people

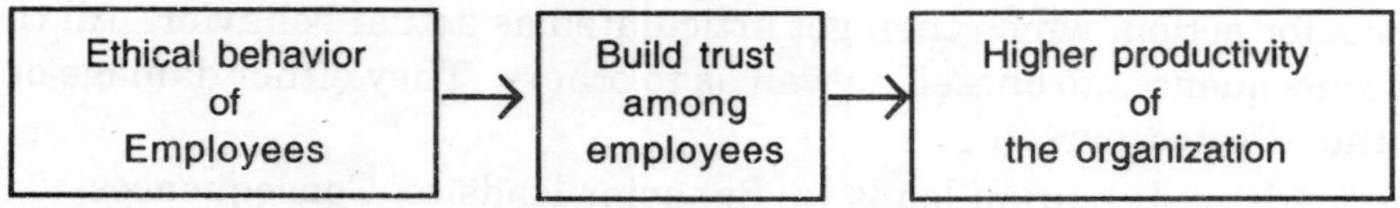

Ethical values involve the behavioral norms and rules that are operant within an enterprise taking the form of an ethical code, covering areas such as conflict of interests, general violating business laws. The attainment of reputation in an organization is based on the ethical behavior and actions of its individuals.

A company's reputation for ethical behavior, its perceived integrity in dealing with customers, suppliers and other stake holders and other parties is a part of company's brand name capital.

Delegation of Decision Rights

Management has to decide properly how to assign decision rights among employee of the company. As decentralization forced companies to leave space for decisions to lower level employees with the multiple benefits of more effective use of local knowledge, saving time of senior management, motivation for lower level management.

Now the question is whether the decision maker has both appropriate information to make good decision and incentives to use information efficiently, or not?

As the employees, who are not the owners, being granted the authority over the use of company's resources and take decisions are less worried about the proper use of company resources than owners. Though managers develop some control system to handle incentive problem, performance evaluation system which help to align the interest of the decision makers with these of the owners. But then also, the managers and employees cannot be mechanically expected to know the suitable decision that promotes the interest of the company.

So there is a need harmonization of values leading to ethical behaviour which means more trust, more productivity, success and reputation.

SUMMARY

Values are deep-seated ideas and feelings. True reflections of one's values are his/her behavior and action. Individual's value formation can be understood in the framework of social psychological theories which have two approaches—Intra-individual and Inter-individual approach. With proper application of knowledge values can be converted in to ethics, the true value of ethical behavior and application can be found by combining ethics and values

QUESTIONS

1. Explain the process of value formation in society.
2. What do you mean by ethical value system?
3. Define values, what are the different types of values.
4. How does value maximization in an organization get affected by ethics?

Part II

Ethics in Organization

Chapter 4

Development of Ethical Corporate Behaviour

- ***Introduction***
- ***Factors Affecting Managerial Work***
- ***Elements Necessary for Ethical Corporate Behaviour***
- ***Summary***
- ***Case Study***

4.1 INTRODUCTION

By the discussion made in the previous chapters, it is clear that how much is the significance of ethics in business.

But now the big question is how to integrate ethics into organization climate. As we know that ethics in management is the discipline which works with what is good or bad and with moral duty and obligation.

According to Clarence Walton—" Managerial ethics is concerned with truth and justice and has a variety of aspects such as expectations of society, fair competition, advertising, public relations, social responsibilities, consumer autonomy and corporate behaviour".

'Koontz and Weihrich' say, "In organizations, managers complete for information's influences and resources. The potential for conflicts in selecting the ends as well as the means to ends is easy to understand and the question of what criteria should guide ethical behaviour becomes acute".

To develop an ethical infrastructure in the organization so many efforts are required. It is not only that top executives are saying, talking advising to follow ethics, so it would be followed. There are some techniques, procedures and steps by which a company can develop ethical corporate behavior.

But before that we have to understand how employees affect the organizations and how organization affects employees.

4.2 "GRIFFIN" EXPLAINED SOME SPECIFIC AREAS WHICH AFFECT MANAGERIAL WORK LIKE

(*A*) Organization towards employees

It covers the areas of wages and working conditions, hiring and firing and employee privacy.

(*B*) Employee towards organization

How employee treat the organization. So many ethical issues are involved, whether any decision which is being made in the favour of the employee and against the company.

Whether employees maintain the honesty and secrecy level or just sell it for their greed.

(*C*) Organization towards other economic institutions

How far organization is fair with its treatment towards other economic agents like stakeholders, suppliers, customers, competition and dealers. The behavior and treatment of all executives towards all stakeholders are dictated by ethical standards.

4.3 ELEMENTS OF PROGRAMMES FOR DEVELOPING ETHICAL CORPORATE BEHAVIOR IN THE ORGANIZATION

(*i*) Ethics Training

To achieve corporate excellence in all the areas and disciplines like sales and Marketing Financial transaction, International transactions, technical systems, purchasing procedures, is the pressing need of this hour. But providing ethics training to employees is a quite new concept. Though some people are under the impression that training in ethics is not possible but we just deny it as so many companies have started their training programmers in ethics like some US companies; General Dynamics, McDonnell Douglas. Every where around the world there is a great need for ethics training properly and carefully designed ethics training programme can make a positive contribution. Though you can't compare ethics training results with other training like technical one in which just after the training you would find the results in the obvious learned knowledge of the trainee, the same will not happen in ethics training but the effects of it would be long lasting.

The basic objectives of ethics training programmer are:

(*a*) To make employees aware of company policy on ethical issues.

(*b*) To train them how to apply and where to apply ethical principles on the job problems everyday.

(*c*) From top to bottom in the organization whosoever faces an ethical question at work is provided with training with the help of simulated case-studies based on actual events in the company.

"**Robert Kreither**"—has provided key features of effective ethics training programme:

- Top management support.
- Open discussion in resolving of realistic cases.
- An organization climate that rewards ethical conduct.
- Inclusion of ethical themes on all training.
- A mechanism for anonymously reporting ethical violations.
- Circulate a copy of code of ethics among all the staff with the explanation about the working procedure and their involvement in it.

(*ii*) Codes of Ethics

A code of ethics basically reflects an organization's primary values, norms beliefs and ethical rules of operations.

Codes of ethics must be framed to encourage ethical behavior in any organization and must be supported by top management. The general practice which is prevalent in our organization the codes of ethics are planned, proposed, discussed and defined by top executives firm and then published and distributed to the staff.

But sometimes the staff members show their reactions to these codes of ethics with doubt, suspicion and believe these norms and beliefs developed in the organization just show the false picture.

"**Cater McNamara**" put forth, "when managing a complex issue, especially in a crisis, having code is critical, continued dialogue and reflection around ethical values produces ethical sensitivity and consensus". The very essential thing is the codes of ethics must be effective.

'Kaptein and Klamer' (1991) had listed some conditions for effective codes of ethics:

(*i*) The introduction must be supported by the important benefits for adopting and complying with the code.

(*ii*) General and broad acceptance of code of ethics must be there.

(*iii*) The process of proper discussion, checking and if needed redefining must be done before the final lay down of codes of ethics.

(*iv*) If we want the implementation and follow up of codes of ethics should become successful event, continuous feed back is necessary.

(*v*) Review, modify, update and if any inconsistency exist between norms, values and practice, it should be disclosed. Further any needed modification and updation should be done.

(*vi*) *Mechanism for control*: For effective enforcement of codes of ethics some system of sanctions must exist. Some examples of corporate codes of ethics are given below:

(*a*) Codes of Ethics for Marketing Managers

(By American marketing Association)

(*i*) Deal with complete honesty and fairness.

(*ii*) In every stage of product development all the standards should be maintained.

(*iii*) Follow all the principles of rights and duties in the process of exchange.

(*iv*) Fair pricing strategy.

(*v*) False, misleading and manipulative promotional tactics must be avoided

(*vi*) Market research must be purposeful and conducted in the manner so that it achieves the objectives.

(*b*) The Engineer's Codes

Some engineer's codes of ethics have been developed by the National Society of Professional Engineers which insist professionals to:

(*i*) Avoid engineering unsafe ventures.

(*ii*) Don't leak the confidential information.

(*iii*) Advise the consequences, if technical suggestion is overruled by a non-technical person.

(*iii*) Organizational Ethics Development System (OEDS)

Some important constituents are:

(*a*) Development of ethics policy handwork and manual for self governance and integrity.

(*b*) Top management commitment which is very important to corporate ethics should be properly communicated.

(*c*) To enjoy the fruits of direct ongoing improvement regular assessment must be conducted of ethics.

(*d*) Sound ethics reporting and conflict resolution process for wrong doers.

(*e*) By Bench Marking to assess individual as well as organization integrity system.

(*iv*) Ethics Committee

Formation of ethics committee is also new concept. In some corporation a standing committee is formed to implement ethical concept into practice, these committees are headed, directed by Board of directors (Internal as well as external):

The salient features and functions of this committee are:

- Periodical assessment.
- Frequent meetings about ethical issues.
- Proper communication about the codes of ethics from top to bottom level.
- Establish reward and punishment system.
- Enforcing the codes.
- Timely reporting to BOD's.

(*v*) Ethics Advocate

An ethics specialist or officer is a member of board of directors who plays a key role to guide for ethical conduct, a good and wide contribution in board's decision making. He shows a correct path to board members as well as other decision makers in the light of ethics.

(*vi*) Integrate Ethical Concepts

The senior level executives have responsibility to apply and integrate ethical concept in day to day actions. They have to build a kind of structure that support ethical behavior like proper information to new employees about ethics standards, annual performance-appraisal, Ethical guidelines and very important system of internal whistle blowing which makes higher management aware of violation in time.

According to **"Purcell and James Weber"** Institutionalizing ethics can be accomplished:

(*i*) By formation of ethics committee.
(*ii*) By providing training in ethics in management development programme.
(*iii*) By Establishing Ethical rules, norms and codes of ethics.

(*vii*) Checklist Method

It has become a new attraction in ethics seminar and workshop. **"Gellermn"** explains that using checklist method employees can avoid the situation when people do unethical behavior justifies it by merely saying like — "It's not really illegal."

"No one will be hurt by it and I will get the benefits".

What to be done when confronted with ethical dilemma for that **"Bennett"** had given some tips:

- Understand and define the dilemma.
- Collect the factual information.
- List out the alternatives.
- Check and test on your standards each alternative.
- Make your decision.

(*viii*) Reward Punishment System

As we know motivation is having a great impact on employees behavior so the best way to get people on ethical path is establishment of reward system. So when ever people behavior is an unethical manner, they do it for some hidden reward so the organization must develop a kind of system in which whosoever shows ethical behavior must be rewarded and whosoever shows unethical behavior must be punished visibly. So for the future conduct people will take lesson and try to act in ethical manners.

(*ix*) Whistle Blowing

Whistle blowing is when an employee tells an employer, who is breaking the law. It was first used for government employees who made complaints to public about corruption and later it was used in private sectors in similar situations.

In true sense in whistle blowing, the employee must tell of the illegal act to someone outside the company. It must be a government or law enforcement agency. Employees who blow the whistle on their employers are protected by laws.

Whistle blowing takes place within an organization and it can be done only day a member/ex-member of an organization.

Whistle blowing can be of two types:

Whistle Blowing

Internal

Report the wrong doing to higher authorities in the same organization.

External

Report the wrong doing of individuals in an organization to external bodies (govt. or private), media, newspaper or public interest groups.

As far as internal whistle blowing is concerned, it is more or less a kind of complaints and sometimes the employee is not protected by the whistle blower laws. However the employee may be protected under other laws for exit is unfair and illegal to fire someone for complaining of sexual harassment or discrimination. If we talk about external whistle blowing not all whistle blowing is equally adversarial to the affected organization, even though it is at least an embarrassment for an organization to be exposed as one that cannot correct its own problems.

There are many regulatory agencies such as OSHO (The Occupational Safety and Health Organization) that exist to perform oversight and to which whistle blowers can go anonymously. But we can see that going to these agencies is usually less adversarial than going to the media.

If the employee has reported the allegedly illegal activity to a government or law-enforcement agency, he or she is protected. The employer cannot retaliate against the employee. The employer cannot mistreat the employee for whistle blowing. In fact it is not necessary that the employer actually broke the law. The employee could be whistle blowing or something that isn't illegal in the first place. The employee is still protected from retaliation or termination but the most important thing in whistle blowing that the employee's belief about violation of law about which he/she is going to blow the whistle must be reasonable.

So, in short, we can say to develop ethical infrastructure in organization, companies must develop some policies regarding whistle blowing like:

- A clearly defined procedure for reporting.
- A guarantee against retaliation.
- An effective communication statement of responsibility for the employees.
- Well trained HR professionals to receive and investigate reports.
- A clear defined procedure for reporting.
- A commitment from higher authority to take appropriate actions.

(X) Other Guidelines

- Establish audit agency reporting to outside directors.
- Practice what you preach should be followed by the leaders of the company.
- Surprise and unpredictable audits.
- Ethics should be evaluated in terms of long range consequences for the individual and the organization.

SUMMARY

In the era of new economy and new ethics, business firms are trying to develop ethical corporate behavior in the organization. Some of the elements which are must to be followed like–ethics training, code of ethics, OEDS, ethics committee, ethics advocate/method, reward, punishment system and whistle blowing in any organization.

CASE STUDY

A company X listed on the NSE (National Stock Exchange) supplies components to company Y. Which further are marketed by company Y in the international market? Since the company Y has stand in the global competitive market, it has signed certain agreement with company X which specifies the company X will use raw materials, from "well known" companies such as "D" and "T".

Instead of buying the raw materials from the reputed companies as per the agreements, company X buys from somewhere else and started bills and test certificates, quite identical to these of 'D' and 'T'. Rajan working as Manager in marketing department of company X came to know about company's unethical practice regarding printed fake bills and providing substandard products to company Y.

He tried to expose the fraud internally and approached to the head of the deptt. As there is a little protection to whistle blowers, Rajan has been fired by his boss. But he did not give up the thing easily. He approached to an external agency "Polo services" to expose the fraud. As the proof of the mischief, he showed some fake bills, test certificates, including an invoice from where they were printed.

Ultimately, Rajan, succeeded to gain the faith of Polo's people. Some experts from "Polo services" approached to company D and company Y. The CEO's of company D deeply scrutinized the bills and provided the proof of the fraud.

After this success Rajan, along with polo's people moved to company Y. They were able to convince the company Y's top executive about the fraud and substandard quality of the components. The company Y had set an internal experts committee to go through the entire case in details.

One month later Rajan, again approached to 'Y' as to find the progress of the case because of which he had lost his job. He had talked with the CEO of company of and was very much disappointed to see the case was all over. CEO tried to make up the things by merely saying that as for as quality is concerned it was found perfectly alright and as company X was facing some problems of excise evasion, law would take its due course. At the end Mr. Rajan regretted about company Y's rejection and was very confused why they haven't taken any action against the fraud?

Comment on the case!

Chapter 5

Ethical Leadership

- ***Introduction***
- ***Leadership-Ethics and Values***
- ***Significance of Ethacal Leadership***
- ***Establish an Ethical Framework***
- ***Summary***
- ***Case Study***

5.1 INTRODUCTION

Leadership is "The ability to influence a group towards the achievements of goals."

Leadership plays a central part towards goal attainment. It is different from management. Good management brings about order and consistency by drawing up formal plans, designing and monitoring results against plans. But leadership is the most important aspect of human behavior. It is about coping with change. They develop a vision of the future, align people by communicating this vision and motivate, inspiring them to overcome hurdles.

Leaders, in 21st century find themselves in a situation where on the one side the pressure is to show excellent results by exploiting opportunities taking into account new technology, globalization, new economy, and on the another side pressure is to discharge social responsibilities, respond to growing expectation and demands among customers.

To operate th· business, companies have social approval and an implicit license received by a no. of stakeholders. This social approval demands from leaders and their companies to do the processes which are consistent with ethical and moral values. As the company gets the permission to operate, so in return it requires satisfying a host of different requirements and expectations.

The following figure reveals that a company collects the license to operate from so many parties involved in the operations.

License to Operate

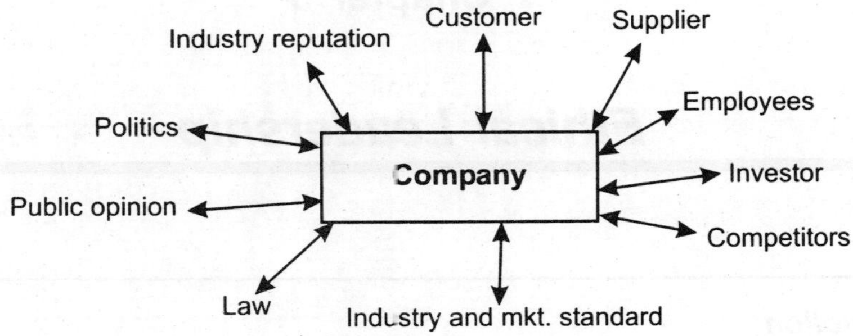

Source: The centre for tomorrow's company.

5.2 LEADERSHIP–ETHICS AND VALUES

Leaders who are able to keep a balance between entrepreneurial skills and corporate citizenship are the effective leaders of the new economy.

Now, true and effective leaders are the one who knows the formula to translate the personal energy of an entrepreneurial leader into the corporate energy of an enduring company.

Here we have a new concept of enduring leadership – which outlasts and transcends the individual, to be a predictor of long term success. Enduring business organizations get return over decades and long term success.

They produce leaders who are "Clock builders" not time tellers. The terms come from 'built to last' a study of leadership and long term shareholder value by 'James Collins' and Jerry Porras of Stanford University. They asked a cross section of American business leaders to identify which companies, not individuals, they admired after 1950, the portfolio of companies they were left with was found to have outperformed the stock market average over 50 years. The main difference between visionary companies and the control group with which they were compared was in their approach to values.

5.3 SIGNIFICANCE OF ETHICAL LEADERSHIP

Effective leadership is about laying the foundations for the efficient and the ethical conduct of business. It is the most powerful and important aspect of human behavior at organizations. If we go through the list of development programmes in corporate world, it ranks at the top. Companies are investing tremendous amount on training for effective leadership because —

(*a*) Long term survival as well as growth starts from ethical leadership, without true and ethical leadership all organizations would be in serious troubles.

(*b*) Integrating ethics into organization needs true leaders. Organization's mission, objectives and goals can be reflected by their vision. They assess the follower's needs and expectations, motivate them, direct them, realise vision. They are the key to communicate organization's values, beliefs.

(*c*) To take organizations on excellence path, a blend of strategy and culture is required which can be achieved by effective leadership. Strategic thinking and cultural building can be built up by leader's moral principles and integrity.

(*d*) Leadership makes real difference between success and failure, whether in a war, a business, games, family or society.

5.4 ESTABLISH AN ETHICAL FRAME WORK

The Co-operative Bank aims to deliver value to all its partners in a balanced fashion over time, where "value" is defined by partners, not the bank. In 2000, the bank produced a pre-tax profit of 90.3 million pounds, an increase of 9% compared with 1999... and the after tax return on equity was 22%. The outstanding commitment of staff is, in my view, probably the single most important reason for this success. In every staff survey conducted. We find quite extra ordinary levels of pride in the bank as the leading promoter of ethical, business practice.

'Mervyn pedelty, CEO, Cooperative Bank'

The Cooperative Bank in UK is one company that has benefited greatly from establishing and adopting an inclusive approach and built up an ethical frame work. Ten years ago the bank stated, defined some relationship on the basis of which it began measuring the impact like surveys for suppliers about their opinion and satisfaction level. The bank actually publishes the results of surveys. Not only this but it also publishes annual reports having information and full details about the value the bank have created for its shareholder customer, staff and society.

The above example states clearly that an Ethical framework which takes an inclusive approach starts with. "Leadership philosophy". A challenge for each and every level of stake holder is to find out what the company orally is, what values, altitudes, are values are the DNA of every organization well defined work values act as a binding force that keeps the work force intact. Some HR experts believe that the organizations culture is the outward demonstration of the values currently existing in the work place, but these questions the way in which some organizations pay lip service and hence dilute "Values" The interpretation of ethical value system for different organizations may vary but should be aptly defined by the leaders. N.V. Sanglikar, senior G.M., Glaxo Smithkline Pharma, India says, "We define our ethics system for the employees as 'total alignment with the company's interest'. This is especially important for the Pharma industry as it is imperative to preserve sensitive information".

It is far more important that values be acceptable to the employees rather than being enforced by seniors. Therefore, it is quite important for the top level management, leaders, to demonstrate the values they preach.

Sydney Fernandez, commercial executive, HR Saatchi and Saatchi advertising adds, "They are role models for their peers and inspire them".

Vaz says, "It's just an empty value system when the top management does not abide with the values themselves. Values then turn out to be mere clichés that need to be left on the corridor walls when you read them."

If a company is advocating something, but the top managers and leader are not following it, practicing it, no employee will respect the system. It is very critical that the senior management set high standards and not assume that values are a corporate sanction. If any of the top executive violates the ethical value system, one should make it known to public, so the other will become aware of disrespecting the ethics of the organization. Accountability is crucial when it comes to using values purposefully. Leaders have an important role to establish the culture in which ethical behavior can be nourished. By setting clearly the purposes and values, achieving universality in diversity, identifying and review the key relationships with stakeholder, a clear cut definition of company's success, measuring the performance and providing appropriate rewards and further proper communication with all stakeholders, leaders can contribute effective in the set of ethical infrastructure.

Now-a-days many organizations believe that a strong ethical value system is indispensable, however it rarely demonstrates what they claim to stand for. To inculcate the right ethics, many leaders use different practices —

For examples, Saatchi and Saatchi have the PIE (Permanently Infatuated Employee) awards every month for the most motivated employee. These awards not only give them a feeling of being acknowledged but also reflect that the organization values people 'who do the right thing and it also sets good example for others to follow'.

Glaxo Smithkline follows a 'Zero tolerance policy' for employee's found disseminating confidential medical information.

At Newgen Software Technologies, every new employee participates in 'Signing in programs' that cover the company's values and describe the employee behavior that go along with lining the Newgen values.

So in short, we say that in 21st century among the epidemic of organizations exposed for shady practices, organization struggle to build a habit of ethical behavior. Many organizations believe that a strong value system is indispensable, however rarely demonstrates what they claim to stand for. Experts believe that each organization has a choice to have a value system that forms the basis of the organizational culture and generates support during crisis management financial dissonance or misuse of intellectual property, or one that is displayed on notice boards to be "followed strictly" but is never implemented.

So how a leader can influence his follower to follow ethics, we have a good example about IBM—

As early as 1961, I circulated a standard of ethics about what our people could and could not do. These were rules against bare - Knuckle selling practices, such as disparaging other companies products or leaking information about machines we hadn't yet announced in order to block a competitor from making sale. Perhaps most important, I told the salesman that in fighting for orders they had to show a sense of fair play. "Tom Walton Junior, president of IBM".

Mr. Walton's 1961 note to salesman includes these words:

"Turn the situation around. Suppose that you were a competitor — small, precariously financed, without a large support organization, and without a big reputation in the field, but with a good product. How would you feel it if the big IBM company took the action which you propose to take".

SUMMARY

Leadership is the most important aspect of human behavior. As a leadership is the ability to influence a group towards achievement of goals so true leadership must be consistent with ethical and moral values. It is an important task for each leader to establish ethical infrastructure in organization.

QUESTIONS

1. What does it mean to be an ethical leader today?
2. Explain the essential steps to establish ethical in organization provided by ethical leaders.

CASE STUDY

Mr. Ashish Gupta completed his MBA from Oxford Business School and returned to India. He joined 'Honda Corporation Ltd.,' a leading company in the Passenger Car Market. He was immediately loaded with the responsibility of regional marketing manager for the western region. Mr. Gupta was an intelligent, dynamic and ethical person.

In the very beginning of his work, he found that some of his subordinates were inefficient, unethical and corrupt. Some of them were used to unduly favoring some dealers.

Some how these subordinates reached the average levels of targets and therefore, the head quarter very often overlooked the activities of these people.

Mr. Ashish tried his level best to correct the situation but he failed. He couldn't understand how to take back his subordinates on the ethical path. He referred some of his books on organization culture, group dynamics and group conflict but afterwards new problem was to correlate "Oxford formula "with Indian situation. He has to keep a balance between his ethical practices and visible corporate success.

Gupta, being an ethical leader, was facing a big challenge to introduce and establish ethical infrastructure in 'Honda Corporation Ltd.'

Suggest appropriate ethical planning to Mr. Ashish Gupta.

Part III

Ethical Choices in Business

Chapter-6

Ethical Decision Making

- ***Introduction***
- ***Ethical Decisions (Individual/Community) in Organization***
- ***Structure of Ethical Decision Making***
- ***How to Use Ethical Reasoning***
- ***Problems in Ethical Decision Making***
- ***Guidelines for Managers for Ethical Decision Making***
- ***Summary***

6.1 INTRODUCTION

As we all know that the real identity of a manager is to make decisions regularly and correctly. As Alvin Toffler says—"The very speed of change introduces a new element into management, forcing managers to make more and more decisions at a faster and faster pace. Now a days management simply has become the process of decision making. All the parts of management pass through decision making toward goal achievement like.

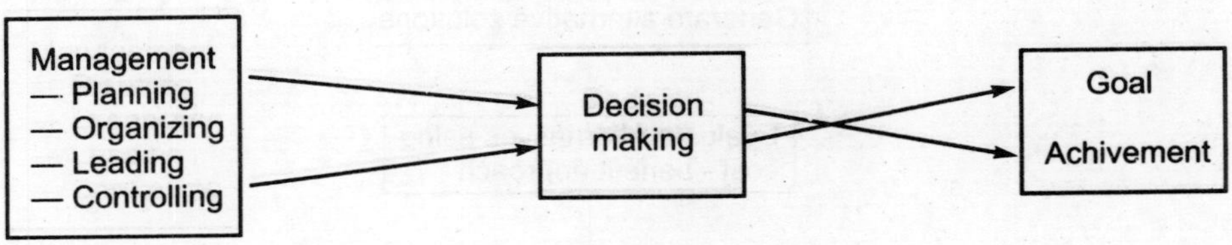

What ever decision of any kind has been taken by any manager has some ethical implications. Here we are going to make the concept ethical decision making clear to the world and show them How Ethics is involved in decision making.

6.2 ETHICAL DECISIONS (INDIVIDUAL/COMMUNITY) IN ORGANIZATION

Most people believe that when they work in group /community, it matters about who are ethical / unethical. They find that if they are ethical by themselves, they might be considered as ethical, or ethically poor or unethical by others.

"Reinhold Niebuhr" (1932), a famous American Theologist, felt that ethical standard fails when Individual work together in a group because their egoistic impulse get compounded. There can be complex psychological reasons for varying levels of ethicality of groups".

The great thinker, Father of Nation, **Gandhiji** also realized and believed in ethics of the means, rather than ends and often tread to lonely path. Tagore too extolled in his famous Bengali poem **"Ekla Chalo Re"** (Strike the lonely furrow). On the other hand "*Karl Kautsky*" (1906, the Marxist philosopher, observed that the larger the conglomeration of people, the higher is their ethicality).

So by seeing this history, we find whether a person works alone or be a part of a group but ethics is in the roots. Neither we can say Tagore philosophy is always right nor we can say karl kutsky's views match with reality.

A typical characteristic of the functioning of a group or organization is that each member has different role to perform. As they perform different functions with different responsibilities so they cannot be evaluated on same yard sticks.

In short, we understand that ethical decision making is a very complex and difficult task. There cannot be a single standard or process which can be followed by each and every one at different stages in an organization. As organizations are not simply mass of people working together but they are an ever present feature of human culture in which persons interact for objectives. The people who work in the organizations are the moral agents, they make collective decisions and act on them, they follow certain rules explicit / implicit, codes of conduct, regulations and their actions based on the followed behavior can be subjected to ethical appraisal.

6.3 STRUCTURE OF ETHICAL DECISION MAKING

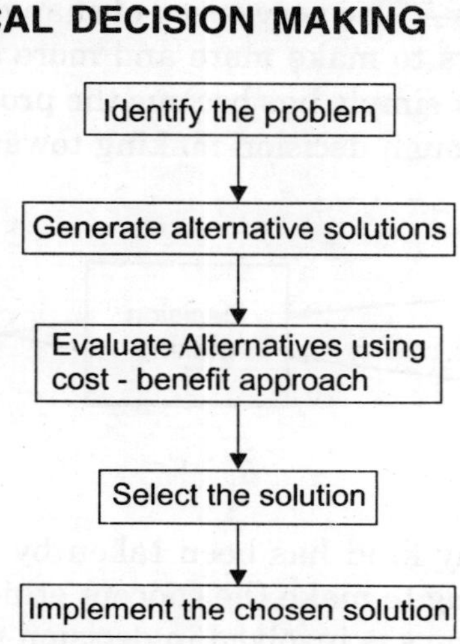

A logical fire steps analytical structure (**Kitson and Campbell 1996**) has been developed to help out the students how they should make the decisions?

Identification of the present situation is the basic foundry and most crucial step. A manager must understand the very nature of the problem or circumstances. Again ethical considerations are involved in alternations generated by decision maker. Now evaluations and selection depend upon so many factors it involves ethical reasoning of the decision maker which is explained in the next part.

6.4 HOW TO USE ETHICAL REASONING

An individual can use the following methods of ethical reasoning:

1. Utilitarian Criteria

This ethical concept was developed by England's "*Jermy Bentham*" and '*John Stuart Mill*' The goal of utilitarian is to provide greatest good for greatest number which is guided by the value, "*Utility*". Decisions are purely made on the basis of their outcomes or consequences.

"It attempted to make ethical evaluation precise by aggregating the happiness of everyone affected and deducting their unhappiness". This is the guiding principle of modern decision making.

To be on safer side decision makers choose utilitarian criteria which helps them to go for some important decisions like termination, closing down plants, laying off large no. of employees, raising prices in the best interest of the organization.

Many people have contradictory view and they argue that perspective needs to change. Therefore further some more criteria have been developed to guide the decision makers to develop ethical standards based on non-utilitarian criteria.

2. Rights Criteria

The focal point of decision making process should be Rights Decisions should be consistent with fundamental rights and liberties as laid in the constitution like-right to speech, right to due process.

Example–As whistle blowing is the latest phenomenon occurring in the modern corporate world of 21st century. So if decision makers use rights criteria, a good protection can be given to whistle blowers, when they blow the whistle against some wrong doers.

3. Distributive Justice Criteria

This ethical reasoning has been given by John Rawls (1971). It sees '*justice*' value as a most likely outcome of an ethical process of decision making. The essential feature of this concept is transparency and full participation of those affected in the decision process.

This requires individuals to impose and enforce rules fairly and impartially, so there is equitable distribution of benefits and costs.

4. Social Contract Criteria

It suggests that empirical and normative or what is and what ought to be must be combined. It integrates two contracts.

1. General social contract among economic participants that defines the ground rules for doing business.
2. A more specific contract among specific members of a community that covers acceptable ways of behaving, so when the managers have to determine what is right wrong they need to look at the existing ethical norms.

Studies have shown that utilitarian is consistent with objectives and goals like efficiency, productivity and high profits.

But because of changing world of management, this opinion, perspective should also be changed. Now society demands to follow non-utilitarian criteria, managers must fix some ethical standards '**Joseph Massie**' says that, "number of generally accepted virtues, such as happiness, lawfulness, consistency, integrity and loyalty, may be in specific situation conflict with one another". Thus managers typically face moral dilemmas in their decisions and actions. He has given two approaches to moral questions —

(i) **Natural law**— This approach considers that certain ultimate values are matters of natural law. Under this view; certain actions are always wrong because they break some basic intuitive law.

(ii) **Situational law**—To determine whether an action is right or wrong, it totally depends upon the situation in which the action occurs. This view holds that an action under one set of circumstances and in one environment would be right, whereas the same action under another set of circumstances and in another environment would be wrong.

So far we have learned bout ethical reasoning; again we come to the structure of decision making.

As in general the most important factors which make the structure of decision making are —

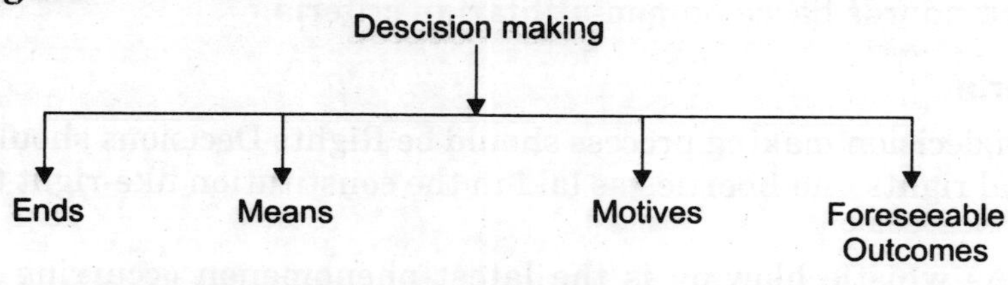

Ethical and unethical actions are largely a function of both the individual's characteristics and the environment in which he works.

The following model explains the ethical/unethical decision making behavior—

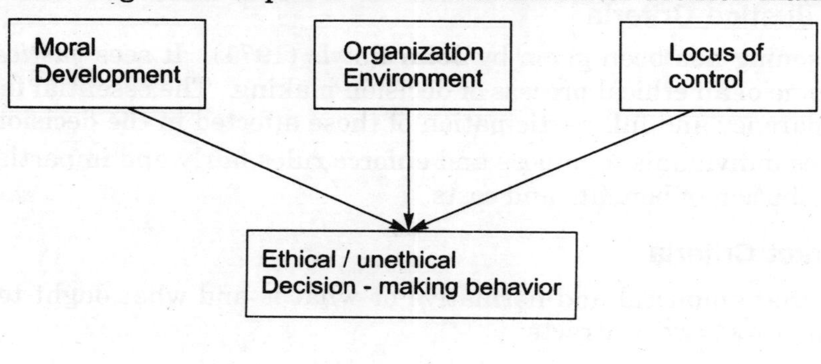

Stage 1: Moral Development

The general belief is that a person's values are formed during his childhood and do not change subsequently. The ability to deal with moral issues develops as they move through their lives.

The process of examining one's moral standards and of applying them to concrete situations includes two parts:

1. A person's ability to use and vertically evaluate his/her moral standards, which develops in the course of person's life.
2. Reasoning processes through which these moral standards are employed and evaluated. The highest one's moral development is the less dependant he is on outside influence.

   For Example — Managers with higher stage of moral development place increased values on the rights of others and regardless of majority's opinion, they are likely to challenge organization practices which they believe are personally wrong.

Stage 2: Organization Environment

Whether the work ethics/organization ethics align with personal ethics. Does the organization encourage and support ethical behavior by rewarding it or discourage unethical behavior by punishing it?

If an individual shows highly ethical behavior at his end and if he finds blanks from organization side, and no valuation of his ethicality, then gradually he will be demotivated towards following ethics. The other side of the coin is a new comer in an ethical organization, though personally not so ethical, slowly moulds in the morally strong environment.

Some examples of these kinds are — high moral behavior by senior management, written codes of ethics, ethics training, performance appraisal, that evaluates every aspects, visible rewards and promotions to whom showing high moral and ethical behavior, simultaneously visible punishment for those who act unethically. All these factors really foster high ethical decision making.

Stage 3: Locus of Control

Locus of control is a particular personality trait which measures the extent to which people believe they are self-responsible for the happenings and events in their lives.

Locus of control

Internal	*External*
Meaning–believes what happens to them in life is fully because of their own actions.	*Meaning*—believes what happens to them is because of luck or chance.
Consequences—believe in themselves; follow their own internal standards of right / wrong to guide the behavior.	*Consequences*—rely on external influence, less likely to take responsibilities.

In short we say that people with strong moral sense, having internal locus of control, are more likely to make ethical decisions.

6.5 PROBLEMS IN ETHICAL DECISION MAKING

It we say or assure that unethical behavior in organization is just because of some wrong doers or some greedy people, some bad individuals who are always behind money, then some where we would be wrong.

Now-a-days, people who look decent, who seem to be ethical, do involve in unethical practices, though they don't think of doing anything illegal or immoral but they get backed into doing some thing unethical by systems and practices of their own firms.

The sources of ethical problems are various and varied:

- Due to globalization, as companies deal with other countries where cross cultural diversity issues arise. Managers working in MNC'S find it very difficult to standardize ethical standards as they do change as society change.
- Some times the decision makers do not follow what they must follow as they have conflict in individual values v/s organizational goals.
- Individual moral standards affect whole organization decisions if they are morally strong, ethical decisions would be the outcomes.
- If the decision makers/managers/policy makers who are greedy, look for short cut routes to earn in earliest possible time, they have an upper hand on the moral values, therefore ethically the decision process would be corrupt.
- Competitive pressure is also the main cause which forces decision makers to choose such path where they have to kill their morals, values and move on unethical path just to cope up with the competition.
- Poor decisions without deep thinking of implications.
- Ambiguous situations create problem which put the manager in dilemma as to which decision they should make and follow.
- Pressures of budget systems.

6.6 GUIDELINES FOR MANAGER FOR ETHICAL DECISION MAKING

1. Individual codes of conduct —
   Here we mean by a man's personal code of ethics. What one finds moral, right and ethical. He/she will choose that option.
2. Industry ethical codes —
   The ethical climate in the industry provides inspirational guidelines and a list of do not's like —
   - Non deceptive ads.
   - Fair dealing with customers
   - Safety measures
   - Quality products.

3. Professional managers who are more ethical do not go for any compromises.
4. Sometimes govt. rules and regulations bound people to follow all laws as well as ethics.
5. Corporate code of ethics —

   Companies own rules, values and beliefs guide managers to follow ethics path in decision making.
6. If the decision makers understand the following process they would definitely follow ethics

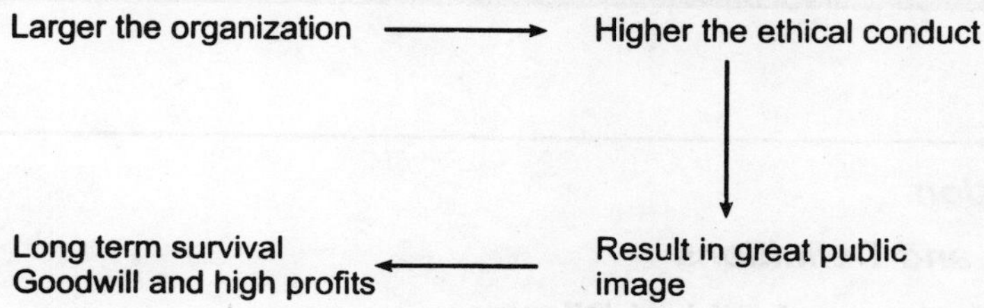

SUMMARY

In the era of globalization ethical decision making has become an important aspect of every organization. Managers by learning a well defined ethical decision making process can make decisions ethically sound. By judging the suitability of utilitarian criteria or right criteria or justice criteria, they should show brilliant ethical reasoning. Though a nos. of problems are emerging as the complexities in business are multiplying, yet some guidelines have been developed to help out the decision makers to make good ethical decisions.

QUESTIONS

1. "People are generally moral agents in an ethical organization". Explain.
2. Discuss the ethical decision making process with suitable examples.
3. Comment on the ethical issues arising out of day to day of business decisions
4. Ethical problems do occur in businesses, explain reasons, sources and some guidelines to mangers to make ethical decisions.

Chapter 7

Ethical Dilemmas in Organisation

- ***Introduction***
- ***Meaning and Definitions***
- ***Salient Features of Ethical Dilemma***
- ***Approaches and Methods of Resolving Ethical Dilemma***
- ***Platinum Standards of Ethics***
- ***Summary***

7.1 INTRODUCTION

When we talk of the problems arising in ethical decision making as discussed in last chapter, we refer to ethical dilemmas, situations in which business men face lots of choices and no clear cut right answer. Businessmen, decision makers do find dilemmas arising out of the eternal conflict between ends and the means. There are easy answers to ethical dilemmas.

Some situations like whether to lie or not, stealing, cheating are easy to be answered but some situations in the practical field when there are so many choices, which seem equally arguable but represent a fake picture of neither clarity nor simplicity. Now let's make this form clear that what ethical dilemmas actually are?

7.2 MEANING AND DEFINITIONS

An ethical dilemma is hard to identify as it is very specific in nature and many situational factors are embedded in it.

Ethical dilemma occurs in the type of situations when one has to choose between right V/s right sorts. Some great men have defined ethical dilemma as —

According to **'Doug Wallace'**— an ethical dilemma exists when one is faced with having to make a choice among following alternatives—

(*a*) Significant value conflict among differing interests.
(*b*) Real alternatives those are equally justifiable.
(*c*) Significant consequences on stakeholders in the situations.

According to '**Rushworth Kidder**'—"In ethical dilemma the toughest choices are right versus right."

'**P. Kidder**' says–"They are genuine dilemmas precisely because each side is firmly rooted in one of our basic, core values four such dilemmas are so common to our experience that they stand as models, patterns or paradigms," they are—

(*i*) Truth versus loyalty
(*ii*) Individual versus community
(*iii*) Short term versus long term
(*iv*) Justice versus mercy.

In general' we say ethical dilemmas are complex judgments on the balance between the economic performance and the social performance of an organization.

Some examples of ethical dilemmas are—

Ramesh Yadav was a marketing officer with a Multinational company. This company used to follow the American system of contributing equally irrespective of their designation. Once, his boss Mr. Anil Sharma invited some office employees out to lunch to celebrate Sunil's Promotion to sales manager. Each employee equally contributed Rs. 175/- for the lunch and the bill was paid by Mr. Sharma. Two days after the lunch Ramesh found out that his boss Mr. Sharma had killed the company for the entire lunch. Now Mr. Yadav is in ethical dilemma, how to handle the situation?

Joseph H. Boyett and Jimmie T. Boyett have cited ethically questionable situations in business as either practices involving out right illegal activities, such as stealing of company's products/practices, misuse of power, application of personal expenses to contract budgets. But these situations offer a clear choice between right or wrong. Ethical issues are just the part of routine practice but they are characterized by less frequent by legal issues. Again dilemma contract with the way ethical issues arise because the basic characteristics are different.

Dilemmas are very specific in nature and hard to identify issues generally easy to name and not specific. Assigning right/wrong, good/bad are quite easy for ethical issues but for dilemma multiple values with multiple opinion what is right for one party may be wrong for the other.

The most important difference between ethical issue and ethical dilemma is when a person finds himself in ethical dilemma, he wants to do the right things but do not know what it is or do not have the capacity to do it but for ethical issue, an individual can do right things if they want to do and have the intentions.

7.3 SALIENT FEATURES OF ETHICAL DILEMMA

An ethical dilemma is very specific in nature and having some special and salient features like—

1. **Uncertain outcomes**

   One can't he sure about the consequences result from most ethical choices.

2. **Multiple choices and Alternatives**

   Like ethical issues in which these are simply two choices 'yes' or 'not' here in ethical dilemma, situations are different decision makers find more than two alternatives which have to be considered.

3. **Mixed consequences**

   Ethical dilemmas and problems in management when solved the out- comes oppose to each other. One decision but considered as favorable by one party and unfavorable by another party, for example, a decision of termination of 10% workforce and increment in the salaries of remaining 90% workforce.

4. **Direct/indirect involvement**

   What will happen to particular situation in which people face ethical dilemma, one side one person is directly involved and on the other side another is just reviewing from distance and not directly involved, obviously ethical decision are more difficult to make when person, personally involved in it.

   For example, what would you do when your immediate boss wants from you to make false TA/DA bills and transfer the benefits to him? So would you follow him or blow the whistle against him? In both the cases you will be in problem.

5. It is a general belief that ethical decisions reduce economic profits of the company but they don't directly impact on managers salary or their other prospectus. So executives sometimes choose the path where profit margin might reduce, keeping themselves on safer sides.

   Thus to conclude we say that ethical dilemmas are very complex in nature. Selection of any one choice among several is quite difficult as well as risky.

7.4 APPROACHES AND METHODS OF RESOLVING ETHICAL DILEMMAS

Infact there are no easy ways, approaches, methods which help practically to resolve ethical dilemma. As the degree of complexity increase, the risk to choose and apply the approaches and methods will become more.

There are some classical approaches and traditional methods develop in resolving ethical dilemmas explained as follows:-

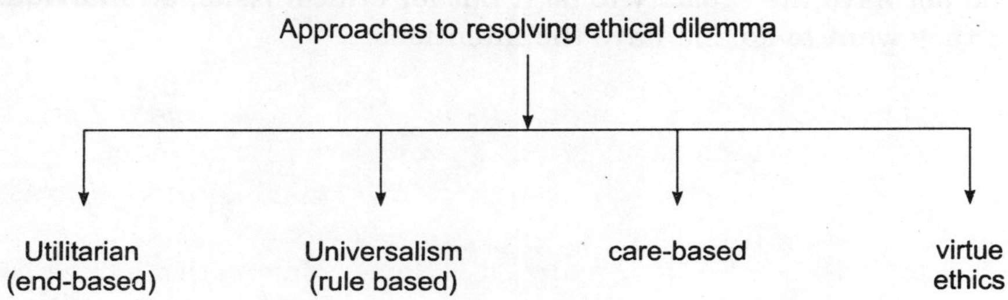

1. Utilitarian (end-based approach)

The utilitarianism system was originated by the British thinker Jeremy Bentham (1748–1832). It aims at creating the greatest degree of benefits for the largest number of people.

According to this system, a human conduct is considered as good if it results in benefits for society and bad if it generates harm to the society.

In-fact Utilitarianism is a special version of "Teleology". Teleology emphasise mainly upon the outcomes of on individual's action and not on the intent of the individual. That's why it is called as "Consequentialism" or end based ethics

2. Universalism (rule based)

The approach of universalism is based on the duties and obligations of an individual (Deontology). The moral worth on individual action should be judged by the intention of the person, not by the outcome of the action. It assumes that good intentions always result in good outcomes, ultimately if not immediately.

'Immanuel Kant' (1724–1804) proposed the "Categorical Imperactive" —

One should act only in ways that one would wish all others to act faced with the same set of circumstances, and also to treat others with dignity and respect. Everyone's value is equal. Hence no one's rights should be subordinated to those of others.

3. Care-based Approach

You have to reserve the dilemma keeping in mind that you have an obligation to care for those with whom you have close relationship or who cares for you. You must care for them just to maintain a strong bond in the relationship but some great-men put some argument against it that it would create favoritism while working with those you have valuable relationship as well as it can degenerate into unjust favoritism and sacrifice of own needs to care for children, parents, spouse and friends with whom you have close relationships.

4. Virtue Ethics

'Peter Partley ' (The essence of business ethics) Says — "Virtue ethics can be represented as a mental construction with prudence. More exactly this metal construction has two ceilings – one is crowned by private prudence and the other by public prudence. The image describes how we can distinguish two sphere of excellence, public and private well being one should make every effort to gain a wider understanding of corporate private and social well being."

Or

In general we say that when a person follows virtue ethics that means while performing any action he/ she should develop a morally virtuous character.

Methods of resolving ethical dilemmas

Ethical dilemmas occur in organization in different forms, framework and structure so single unique and standard method can not be applied to resolve them.

Each and every organization has its own strategies, planned procedure for dealing with ethical dilemma. Generally a committee of top level managers is being setup to select suitable approach and method to solve ethical dilemma. Some methods have been given by great men like –

1. 'Rushworth Kidder'– A nine steps procedure for dealing with ethical dilemma.
2. 'Wallace and Pakel'– Ten steps of decision making.
3. 'Laura L. Nash' – Presented twelve questions to address ethical dilemmas.
4. Nine steps for dealing with ethical dilemma (by Rushworth Kidder) (extract from how good people make choices - "Resolving the dilemmas of ethical living, William/ Morrow, New York, 1995).
   1. Define the problem and clearly recognize the moral issues in it.
   2. Determine who will affect by the decisions? What would be your role?
   3. Until and unless ethical dilemmas can be reduced to common issues which are though difficult but manageable it is hard to resolve them for this one has to collect the information and facts how the problem occurred.
   4. Isolate the illegal issues involved in the problem by testing right versus wrong.
   5. Now the time has come to make the toughest choice which is right versus right paradigms such as —
      Justice V/s mercy
      Short term V/s long term
      Truth V/s loyalty
      Individual V/s community
   6. At this stage you can select any one appropriate approach to resolve dilemma like
      - Care based
      - Rule based
      - End based

      or virtue ethics (already discussed earlier)
   7. Find out if there is any another way out of situations.
   8. Decide and Act — finally select an approach which you find the most suitable, decide that and take action.
   9. Review of the decision—

   Apart from these (mentioned above) methods 'Hosmer' has given five things which should be followed to make ethical issues and dilemmas much simpler than ever—

   (*i*) The decisions taken by managers must be with intense care as their consequences may affect the organization as well as the society.

   (*ii*) Ethical choices are full of mixed outcomes. One side social benefits and other side financial revenue.

   (*iii*) If you see from an upper layer you will find there are clear cut two alternatives 'Yes' or 'not' but actually most of the ethical issuer have multiple alternatives equally arguable.

   (*iv*) How ethical decisions and personal implications are related with each other?
   Mostly ethical decisions have personal implications though the common belief says ethical decisions are isolated from executive's careers.

(*v*) The degree of uncertainty is very high in ethical issues, uncertain consequences with full of risks and doubts are embedded in ethical decisions.

7.5 PLATINUM STANDARD OF ETHICS

'Scoft W. Ventrella' (Executive excellence, July, 2001) provides a platinum standard of ethics for dealing with ethical dilemma as follows :

1. Ask yourself— Whose problem it is? Is it a case of conflicting interests or a question of right and fairness? In the ' Power of Ethical Management 'Norman Vincent Peale and Ken Blanchard ask:
   (*i*) Is it legal or illegal? What you are doing is in line with policy or against policy then don't do it and.
   (*ii*) How much fairness is there? If it provides benefits to few one, don't do it.
   (*iii*) At the end what is my self analysis? How will I feel about myself?
2. Does the decision accurately reflect the kind of person you are? Does your character match your decisions? Do you follow—Practice what you preach?
3. Be careful and aware of what actions you show and try to imagine the situations that if all your deals, actions, phone calls being observed, recorded and further reported what would be the outcomes.
4. Keep your words – How firmly you fulfill your commitment. Is it the way you make promises lightly, sometimes fulfills and sometimes not. If so then some practices will be followed by your subordinates and associates. So try to say no it you can't complete it or don't want to complete it or do not know how to do it.
5. Develop and Sustain integrity – The most powerful value is integrity which is–
   - Courage (telling the truth).
   - Self discipline and control.
   - Goodness—honesty, morality, kindness, fairness, generosity.
   - Centering power—which provides us with the navigational tools, how to pass the fuzzy ethical landscape.
   - Living by inner truth and inner mind to remain yourself incorruptible, clean from kick-backs etc. let your mind be guided by conscience.

SUMMARY

Ethical dilemmas are the particular situations in which decision makers face difficult choices with no clear-cut right answers exist. Because of some special and different features like uncertain consequences, multiple alternatives etc. Managers and executives have to be very careful handling ethical dilemmas. Though some traditional methods have been developed which help decision makers to handle the complex situations and make an ethical decision.

QUESTIONS

1. What is an ethical dilemma, explain?
2. Ethical dilemmas are more complex in nature than ethical Issues, comment.
3. What do you mean by platinum standards of ethics? Explain it with some examples.

CASE STUDY-1

Mr. Rahul Tandon, VP (HRM) for a manufacturing firm 'XYZ.' The firm is undergoing a major change in direction. The rapid changes in the Industries as well as competitors dynamic policies and plans, put a big pressure over the firm to adapt in the new environment. In this changing environment, Mr. Tandon is thinking of hiring some young, energetic and advanced persons who would be able to cope up the dynamic and changing situation. 'XYZ' has organized a walk in interview for new recruitments Ms. Isha Patil, well qualified as well as experienced in the similar field has appeared for the interview. She has just left one of the competitor's company because of some personal reasons. Meanwhile in the interview she indirectly gave the hints that she would be happier to tell you all the competitors' plans and policies.

What would Mr. Tandon do?

CASE STUDY-2

Mr. Rakesh Sinha was working as an officer in the excise deptt. of a reputed steel company. He was from a very reputed and good family.

The steel company was reportedly involved in excise evasion of its goods. Excise evasion by the company resulting in dealer selling steel which was not excise paid. Mr. Sinha along with his boss were directly involved in excise evasion. Their philosophy being that, they are doing it not for good of their own but for the company.

The govt. had recently raided few companies practicing excise evasion lying in the vicinity of the steel company. Therefore, Mr. Sinha was under tremendous stress these days. Even he knew that his name would come in the list, as one of the company's executive to be interrogated. Mr. Sinha's wife, knowing about the entire situation advised him to get out of such activity or else quit the company.

Mr. Sinha was in dilemma, what should he do?

Part IV

Corporate Social Responsibilities

Chapter 8

Social Responsibility of Business

- *Introduction*
- *Meaning and Definiton*
- *Why Business Should be Socially Responsible*
- *Social Responsibilities Models*
- *Main Social Responsibilities of Business Organization*
- *Corporate Social Responsibility and India*
- *Summary*

8.1 INTRODUCTION

It can be said with confidence that business isn't what it used to be. It is changing radically as a result of major societal forces such as technological advances, globalization etc.

Business depends upon society for the inputs like manpower, resources, money etc. The very existence, survival and growth of any firm depend upon its acceptance by society and its environment. Business organizations have to earn social sanctions without which they will collapse and die out simultaneously as they exercise a remarkable influence on our socioeconomic life style, they must understand their responsiveness towards society.

In this modern era, society is expecting much more from business than in the past. Business firms are now no longer considered as economic institutions, they are now socio – economic institution where basic reason to exist is not merely earning profit. Though profit making is the basic objective of any business and with out it, it wouldn't survive, but the concept of profitability has been changed. Now profit in terms of goodwill creditability and trust of society is more valuable than profit in terms of money or return on investments. The image of a company depends upon service and satisfaction of the people. The long term survival of a company is possible when a company does what is favorable to the society and in the interest of the customers, it serves.

8.2 MEANING AND DEFINITION

Corporate social Responsibility is not a new fangled buzzword. An organization influence over employees, customers, partners, shareholders, the community and the environment cannot be overstated. CSR activities and programs are now quite an integral part of organizational objectives.

'Keith Devis' in "can business afford to ignore social Responsibilities?" California Management Review, 1960, defined social responsibility as —

"Social Responsibilities refer to business man's decisions and actions taken for reasons at least partially beyond the firm's direct economic or technical interest".

Social Responsibility is thus an obligation of decision makers to take actions which protects and improve the welfare of society as a whole along with their own interest.

CSR is one of the prime focus areas of an organization. The benefits from all such efforts and endeavors the company shows in the development of society should trickle down to as many people as possible long back in 1963.

Management guru **Peter F. Drucker** stated the relationship between organization and society in his book 'practice of management'- "is like the relationship between a ship and the sea which Ingrid's it and carries, which threatens it with storms and ship wreck which has to be crossed but which is yet alien and distant, the environment rather than the home of the ship. But society is not just the environment of the enterprise. Even the most private of private enterprises is an organ of society and serves a social function".

"The responsibility of management in our society is not only for the enterprise itself, but for management's public standing, its success and status, for the very future of our economy and social system and the survival of the enterprise as an autonomous institutions. The public responsibilities of business must therefore underline all its behavior. Basically it furnishes ethics of management".

'L.N. Prasad in ' Principal and practices of management gave an operational definition of social responsibility "Social responsibility contends that management is responsible to the organization to the organization itself and to all the interest groups with which it interacts Other interest groups such as workers, customers, creditors, suppliers, govt. and society in general are placed essentially equal with shareholders".

Extracts from a speech by Mr. Mukesh Ambani (Chairman, RIL), published in Times of India (15th Nov., 2002), he expressed his views based upon his own practical experiences on the relationship between business and society -

"Business in our culture is not merely an activity for Individual profit. In the Indian Milieu, a business person is a custodian of the vital interest of society".

'*Mahatma Gandhi*' articulated this view in his inimitable way. He called on business leaders to consider themselves as trustees of society's wealth. Given this back ground the concept of social partnership comes naturally to us".

Further he added– "Responsible companies now present triple bottom lines in their annual report- financial, environmental and social. Financial investors increasing take a negative view of socially irresponsible companies and shy away from 'Sin stoks' of course, this is not enough. Even now society and business are viewed as two district activities trying to engage each other. That is far cry from true and vibrant partnership. Therefore much more needs to be done. Business and NGOs still relate to each other in a confrontation mode. This must change".

In a nutshell from the above discussion we understand corporation should look forward to long term relations with the community where life it touches.

A corporation must understand that the time and resources thus invested and the, professional expertise shared with the nation comes back to the corporation in the long run as expected dividends of reputations, opportunity and acceptance.

8.3 WHY BUSINESS SHOULD BE SOCIALLY RESPONSIBLE

A common question regarding why business men should be socially responsible! What visible on invisible benefits they will enjoy being socially responsible? What differences they will generate with when who are socially irresponsible? Some genuine reasons are as follows:

1. Long Term Survival

If an organization wants to survive in the long run, it has to establish a loyal brand of customers, repeat customers etc. Suppose if they do harm to the society by their irresponsible conducts, society will not allow them to exit in the future.

2. Public Expectation

General public requires certain behavior from organization apart from quality products, fair prices, good services etc.While doing the businesses they should not disturb any balance of society like (pollution, crimes, corruption etc.)

3. Goodwill

As we know that goodwill cannot be begged or borrowed, it can be earned and it will happen when the organizations will understand and discharge their social responsibilities.

4. Govt. Laws and Regulations

Some times the govt. laws and regulations force the business organization to behave in socially responsible manner to survive in long run.

5. Better Environment to Operate

If an organization can improve the quality of life of customers, try to integrate private good and public good, more concentration on solving a particular problem of the society, automatically better it is able to solve its own problem and in better environment it will get to operate.

6. Keep the Balance (Give and Take Relationship)

Business organization exists and operates with in society. As it takes so much from society, so it also owes something to the society. When business men understand the fact that they are social entities, with out society's approval they wouldn't exist, they accept their responsibilities towards society and attempt to fulfill them.

8.4 SOCIAL RESPONSIBILITIES MODELS

The interlink ages of business and society by system approach—

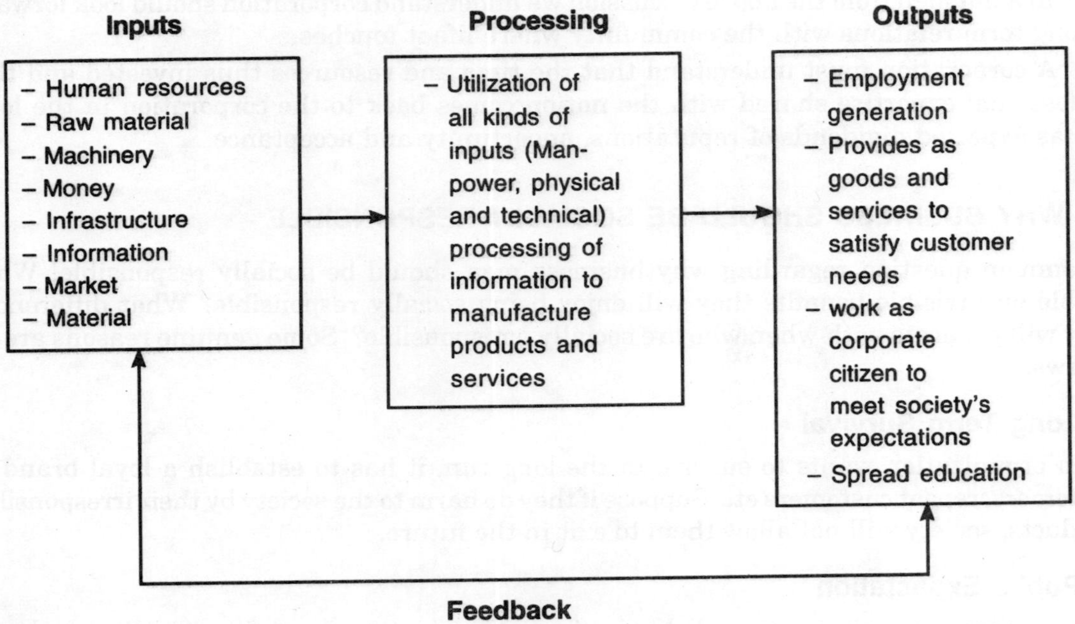

As from above representation it is clear that business is part of larger social system. Any business takes inputs from society, does its processing and provides the outputs to the same society. So the outputs must be acceptable as well as desirable to the society. So the mutual understanding and interactions between society and business must be very sound.

The contribution which business makes to society and vis-a-vis is very significant. So if the outputs of the processing are not up to the satisfaction level of society, some preplanning must be done till the desired results are accomplished.

So we say business is not considered economic institution and should be considered as a social institution.

To understand social responsibility technically some models have been developed by some great man. Some of which are presented as follows to make us understand each and every aspect of social responsibility –

1. Ackerman's Model of Social Responsibility

Ackerman insists and suggest that the basic goal of any corporate entity should be social responsiveness. When firm decides to be social responsible it has to pass some developing stages like –

Awareness stage

↓

Planning and action stage

↓

Implementation stage

In the beginning of the process the top managers and decision makers must learn of an existing social problem. The key players generally are MD or CEO of the company. Once identification about the existing situation is over proper and adequate planning should be done for this it requires the firm must hire some specialist or consultant so there would be no loopholes in the planning stage. The most effective stage is to implement all the planning. Implementation should be of such kind that it would become an integral part of daily operations. A true commitment through out all the levels of organizations must be obtained.

2. Carroll's Model of Social Responsibility

According to Carroll's, there are four categories of social responsibilities of business :

(*a*) Economic responsibilities –

The basic and primary responsibility of any business is to be economic. Producing goods and services to satisfy society's needs and wants and generate profit by selling them.

(*b*) Legal Responsibilities –

Each and every business entity must operate with in the law and legal frame work; these are considered as legal responsibilities.

(*c*) Ethical Responsibilities –

As in the earlier chapter the difference between ethics and laws already explained so here being ethical responsible means doing according to the expectations of society might be not codified in a law.

(*d*) Discretionary Responsibilities –

Discretionary responsibilities are steps forward of ethical responsibilities, in which firms go for voluntary actions to serve society. Society will not demand to be discretionary responsive, it is the firm's willingness to contribute something in the welfareness of society.

3. Approaches to Social Responsibility

'Gene Burton and Manab Thakur' (Management today) have provided some social responsibilities strategies which explained a ladder of degree of social responsibility.

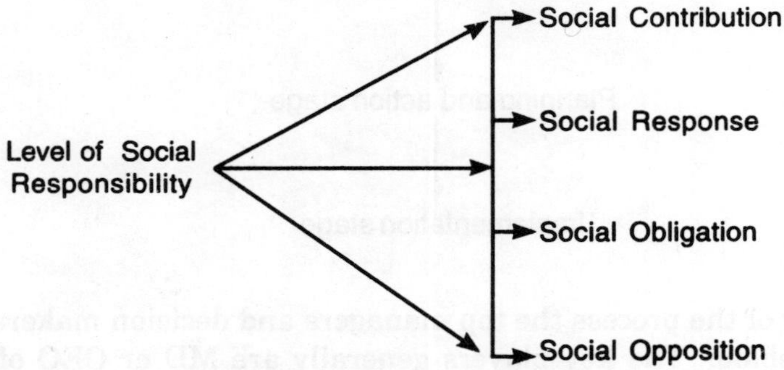

(*i*) Social opposition –

When businesses opposing the society by feeling or showing no obligations towards it, it is called social opposition. If while doing any unethical act they are being caught, they make themselves safe by denying it or some other practices like bribery.

(*ii*) Social obligation –

The firms in this category believe that as they are operating in society so it is their duty to do business in the legal boundaries.

(*iii*) Social Response –

The firms in this degree do little more than social obligations. They realize that merely fulfilling legal requirements are not sufficient right now. So they go beyond, towards ethically conduct of business.

(*iv*) Social contribution –

The firms which contribute themselves to social development fall in this category. It is the top most steps on the ladder of socially responsiveness. They do their business via fully dedication and committed to society.

8.5 MAIN SOCIAL RESPONSIBILITIES OF BUSINESS ORGANIZATION

Though the list of social responsibilities should be discharged by business organizations is a long one yet some major responsibilities which cover all the basic parts are as follows —

1. Responsibility to Make Profit

The basic objective of any business should be to earn profit. As a loss making organization cannot produce quality products, cannot fulfill its commitments, cannot generate revenue for share holders etc. So, organizations have a social responsibility to be profitable, and then only it will be able to meet its social obligations and expectation.

2. Responsibility to Generate Employment

Every business must provide fair opportunities to all the people. They must create the conditions and situations which help the employees to put forward their best efforts to achieve organizations goals.

3. Responsibility of Optimum Untilization of Resources

Each organization must understand that it has some moral obligations to utilize the scarce national resources of the country in an optimum way, not to waste, damage or mis-utilize of the resources.

4. Responsibility to Provide Quality Products

Providing quality products at fair prices is one of the important social responsibilities. If the service given by the product meets with the customer expectations and also they find products are available at fair prices, they will feel satisfied.

5. Responsibility to Protect the Environment

Protection of the environment is equally important as other responsibilities. Business organizations are the responsible corporate citizens so they must take serious and responsible steps to protect the environment and keep it in a healthy condition.

6. Responsibility to Provide Quality of Life

Quality of life is one's internal growth, growth of character, mind and soul and enriched life. So business firms should provide opportunities to its employees as well as to society to enrich their lives and better quality of life.

7. Responsibility to Safeguard the Health

Safeguard the health and physical safety of consumers as well as employees become as vital area to be cared by the organizations. This becomes more serious with drug and cosmetic companies. They must take adequate care to check and safeguard consumer's health and well being.

8. Fair Trade Practices

If business firms are showing socially responsible behavior they must go for fair trade practices some of which like – not making false advertisements, avoid monopolistic trade practices, not go for artificial scarcity, not bribing public servants, quality products, fair prices, provide timely and accurate information to its stakeholders etc.

9. Responsibility to Development of Nation

If companies are involved in international businesses, they must contribute their effort towards development of their country by earning foreign currency, earning goodwill and reputation in global market, make good relationship among nations etc.

10. Responsibility to Fulfill all Duties and National Obligation

As corporate citizen, business firms are required to fulfill certain obligations under various laws and to perform certain duties. They must operate their business within the boundaries of legal framework provided by govt. they must contribute to national prosperity and try to reduce some national problems like corruption, unemployment etc.

8.6 CORPORATE SOCIAL RESPONSIBILITY AND INDIA

Corporate social responsibility activities and programes are now quite an integral part of organizational objectives. In the last 14 years since liberalization Indian companies has come to terms with CSR and its wider ramification.

Whether we talk about private sector or public sector most of all have accepted social responsibility of business as part and parcel of their economic activities.

Some of the PSU (Public Sector Undertakings) have been more active in the field of CSR. OIL (Oil India Ltd.) is one company among them. It is an Indian oil drilling company which is associated with community and society development, by providing low-cost housing, building Schools and Colleges offering monetary help to financially weaker students etc.

NTPC (National thermal power corporation) is the first PSU in the country to have developed a comprehensive R and R policy, while even the Government of India has been still working on a national policy. It's also one of the rare Indian organizations to have a clearly articulated corporate social responsibility policy.

The Main CSR Policies of NTPC are

- To lead the sector in the areas of resettlement and rehabilitation and environment protection including effective ash-utilization, peripheral development and energy conservation practices.
- To continuously attract and develop competent and committed human resources to match standards
- 0.5% of its profits are set aside for community development measures under the umbrella of CSR.
- To contribute to sustainable power development by discharging CSR.

Indian private companies are also showing their brilliant efforts in CSR activities.

We start with Tata group of companies whose belief is shaping a society with social purposes, Jamshedji Tata, the founder of Tata group and his sons believed that the real purpose of industry was to go beyond the creation of wealth to the building of a new society through the proper allocation of that wealth. It was from this vision Tata institute of social science was born.

JRD Tata conducted his business in a very socially responsible way. He wanted to bring an industrial revolution to an economically back ward India. The very specific goals of JRD Tata at that time were to establish a hydro electric power project at Bombay as a cheap source of energy, the steel industry at Jamshedpur and Indian institute of science at Banglore to provide technical education.

Ratan Tata in One Interview Expressed his Views like

"Ethics for Tatas means conducting business in manner which is fair and just to employees, suppliers and shareholders; having a concern for the community in which one is operating. It would involve putting combined interests above personal gain or exploitation".

India's premier air conditioning and engineering service provider Voltas limited has paid more than lip service to CSR. The company is committed to facilitating the development of a strong self reliant community and has a well defined framework for implementing its community development agenda. As Voltas, true to Tata traditions of improving quality of life, has long regarded participation in social development as a whole hearted pre-occupation that enriches the corporation itself.

Voltas is moving towards exhibiting their true corporate citizenship through the triple bottom line concept–economic, environmental and social.

- The Mafatlal Group of industries is also moving towards discharging corporate social responsibilities like engaging in rural welfare activities, providing drinking water, distributing books, stationary and scholarship to students in rural areas.
- ACC (Associated Cement Companies) started their efforts in this direction three decades back. It launched a village welfare scheme in 1952 and continuing with setting up schools, colleges, health centers and co-operative societies with the intention to provide employment and improving the quality of rural life.
- MUL (Maruti Udyog Ltd.) is another example of an Indian organization highly profitable being socially responsible economic entities.
- Infosys Technologies Ltd. has also been discharging its social responsibilities. Being very transparent corporation, this company became the first Indian company in 1997 to prepare its accounts in compliance with the US generally accepted Accounting practices and Securities Exchange Commission disclosure norms. The CEO of this company says," from day one, we recognized that, to succeed, we had do operate on certain principle, and having decided to go public, we must be sure that wealth is created within the business.
- HDFC (Housing Development Finance Corporation) has also been working as true corporate citizen of India since long back. In 1996, its CEO was awarded by the JRD Tata corporate leadership award by All India Management Association (AIMA) in recognition of their corporate excellence through socially responsible activities.
- Another public sector giant Bharat Petroleum Corporation Ltd. (BPCL) is showing brilliant efforts in CSR activities. They have adopted 37 villages all over India. Their programme for vocational training and agricultural innovations with improved know how have helped villagers increase their income levels. The underlying philosophy which drives CSR activities at BPCL is about society and nation building.

SUMMARY

Business organization must discharge their social responsibilities. To exist and operate with in the social structure they must fulfill their social obligation along with economic obligations. There are some models and Approaches have been developed by some great men to understand and implement social responsibility strategies in different segment of business enterpriser. The major social responsibilities are – responsibility to earn profit, provide quality product, fair trade practices, optimum utilization of resources, environmental protection, quality of life, take care of health and safety of society etc. Many organizations now a days have accepted social responsibility of business and therefore showing their great efforts in discharging the responsibility.

QUESTIONS

1. Why business must be socially responsible? Explain.
2. Define and explain the term corporate social responsibility.
3. Explain the various social responsibility models.
4. What are the major areas in which a firm should be socially responsible?
5. Comment on some socially responsible Indian companies and their activities.
6. Discuss 'whether social responsibility of business 'a fair practice or a game for frame.

Chapter 9

Corporate Governance

- ***Introduction***
- ***Historical Background***
- ***Factors Behind the Origin***
- ***Important Issues of Corporate Governance***
- ***Corporate Governance in India***
- ***Professionalisation of Corporate Governance***
- ***How to Achieve Good Corporate Governance***
- ***Summary***

9.1 INTRODUCTION

Corporate means legally united into a body so as to act as an individual and governance is not but the dissection or control.

So corporate + Governance = Corporate Governance is nothing but the way by which corporation are controlled and directed. As corporation brings together different groups like employees, suppliers, customers, invertors, govt.– to carry out the business conduct these entire group interact, corporate, contribute with each other. They are vital for the existence, survival and growth of the business. So corporations should be operated for the benefits of all these stakeholders (customers, employees, suppliers, society, govt., investor etc.) A single business entity and involvement of such multiple groups, it means brilliant governance is required. Here we are not talking about managing or ownership, the need is for governing which is different from merely ownership. The term 'corporate governance' refers to the guidelines, procedures, rules for decision making, means of achieving targets on corporate affairs. It also suggests how to monitor the performance.

'**Sir Adrian Cadbury**' has defined corporate governance as– "corporate governance basically has to do with power and accountability; who exercise power, on behalf of whom and how the exercise of power is controlled..."

A great man says about it like,– "corporate governance is a conscious, deliberate and sustained efforts on the part of corporate entity to strike a judicious balance between its own interest and the interest of various constituents on the environment in which it is operating".

9.2 HISTORICAL BACKGROUND

The origin of corporate governance took place in the U.K. in 1990. Some recommendations had been given by a committee headed by Sir, Adrian Cadbury in corporate governance. He had explained the basic and primary factors, drives behind corporate governance in the U.K. like –

(*a*) The majority of shares were from Institutions rather than individuals. Institutional invertors like pension funds owned big amount of capital which represent the savings and pensions of lakh of people so if the company is not being managed well the needy people would be in trouble.

(*b*) As global operations were speeded up, it came up as a tool to attract foreign investment.

(*c*) Because of competitive pressure, the no. of fraud cases, falsify accounts and unethical practices were increasing.

(*d*) It was thought that the companies would under mine the social, ethical and environmental concern in the era of privatization.

If we move in flashback, around 1990s in India a quite similar situations were developing under three major happenings –

- Liberalization
- Privatization
- Globalization

Indians had opened the door for whole globe firms started accessing the funds from all over the world.

9.3 FACTORS BEHIND THE ORIGIN OF CORPORATE GOVERNANCE

In today's changing face of corporate world, a proper balance between people's aspiration and business demands could be achieved with the implementation of good corporate governance that give presence to the human element in the organizations, mainly focus on people centered policies. The philosophy of corporate governance aims not only for achieving business goods but also to maintain the sustainability in profit and human values.

In the cutthroat competitive world, global firms have to evolve with innovative strategies aimed at staking their claims in the increased pool of profits, bringing values to the contribution of the share holders, suppliers, employees of the firm and customers.

Now a days so many companies have established elaborate systems, well defined structures, highlighting their practices of corporate governance in annual publishing for these rapid changes and there are some special reasons like –

(*a*) In the globalization era, when expansion, innovation diversification of the business is going on very fast. Foreign investors have become very careful about investing their money. So to attract foreign investment more and more and to raise capital in International Mkt., you need a sound practice of corporate governance.

(*b*) Government of India has also implemented strict rules and laws to be followed, like Kumar Mangalam Birla committed appointed by SEBI, some professional CII Codes etc.

(*c*) The nos. of institutional investors has increased so there is a felt need to safe guard their interest.

(*d*) The increasing active rate of investigating reporting in business journalism.

(*e*) No.´ of International events (like joint ventures, mergers, takeovers) in the wake of globalization are taking place so it is required that proper corporate governance practices should be followed.

9.4 IMPORTANT ISSUES OF CORPORATE GOVERNANCE

The major issues related to corporate governance are –

1. Social responsibility
2. Multiple, divergent expectations of shareholders,
3. Only economic obligations or social and environmental obligations are also important for organizations.
4. Fair business deals, corruption.

In a lecture to the stern school of business, New York on 26.03.2002 Mr. Alan Greenspan, Chairman of the Federal Reserve Board made the following points –

- As economy has grown, de-facto shareholder control has diminished.
- CEO sets business strategy, selects auditors, and determines accounting practices.
- Few directors have seen their interests as different from that of the CEO.
- Directors who are independent of CEO's influence would create competing power center with in a corporation and dilute control and impair effective governance.
- Rapid technological change makes it difficult to assess and project profit opportunities. Short term results are used to project long term views. Therefore auditors have sanctioned accounting devices whose sole purpose is to obscure potential adverse results.

9.5 CORPORATE GOVERNANCE IN INDIA

The corporate world in India can be divided in to two parts:

- Private sector
- Public sector

So to understand the corporate governance practices in India we have to learn about the sector's structure, categories of shareholders, their working patterns etc.

I. Private Sector

In India, for private sectors, the broad categories of shareholders are:

- Promoters
- Financial Institutions
- Individual investors.

All these three categories are equally important and any private enterprise's board comprises of three types of directors—

(*a*) *Promoter director*–Called as functional director and belong from promoter group.

(*b*) *Professional director*–A category of directors who are invited by promoter group on the basis of favorable personal equation.

(*c*) *Institutionally nominated*–These positions are fulfilled by senior executives or person of good image and reputation.

For electing the directors, typically in India, we follow majority rule voting system.

The role of institutional investors is very limited, they support the promoters. They only make their interference when crisis occurs or they find any malafide behaviour on the part of Mgmt.

In our country we find there are some private banks like ICICI, UTI or IDBI, which frequently guide advice and some times force the companies to undertake restructuring initiatives aimed at protecting the interest of institutional investors.

In India, so corporate governance in private sector is characterized as 'entrenched system' given the firm hold of the promoters over the companies managed by them.

II. Public Sector

The firms, companies where equity shares are owned wholly (51% or more) by government of India (in the name of the president of India) are in the category of public sector or we name them PSU'S (Public sector undertakings) the board of public sector, has been appointed by the controlling administrative ministry for all practical purpose. Mainly we divide the board in 3 parts.

(*a*) Functional directors–Functional directors are the full time employees of the PSUS.

(*b*) Govt. directors–They are the bureaucrats from different controlling administrative ministry.

(*c*) Out side directors–If we compare the working procedures and styles between private sectors and PSUS, we find public sector is far behind than private sector. Bureaucratic and political influence is embedded in the roots of management of PSU'S, such that autonomy is often eroded. Delegations of power authority, freedom to take decisions are generally not present in PSU'S environment. Therefore many administrative guidelines, regulations are present in day to day working, that are subject to the CAG audit (controller and auditor general) and also they are accountable to the parliament which leads to an excessive emphasis on observing rules, regulations and guidelines.

The most important thing which makes PSU's weak, less effective is the short tenure of chief executive of public sector undertakings. They generally are appointed for one to five years. So it is very rare to find a visionary leader, guiding the destiny of a PSU with a long planning horizon. The consequence of such a short tenure with limited freedom is the myopic outlooks of CEO's. They involve only in fulfilling the short term targets and completing the terms and conditions of memorandum of understanding (MOU). All these lead to low compensation level, poor incentives, soft performance standards and weak accountability.

9.6 PROFESSIONALISATION OF CORPORATE GOVERNANCE

As the above discussion makes it clear to India that the standards of corporate governance are not up to mark, there is a pressing need for reforms. Some ways of reforming corporate governance in practice that have been developed are as follows:

1. Distinguish Management from Control

The Cadbury committee report say, "The board should retain full and effective control over the company and monitor the executive management".

It means that there must be a separation between control and management.

Eugene fama and Michel Jensen suggest four distinguished components under management and control.

Control	*Management*
– Ratification (Proposals developed in the initiations stage are evaluated, if suitable, and then approved. – Monitoring (Assessment of executive's performance and implementation of proper reward system.)	– Initiation (Proposals for managing the resources of the firms are developed) – Implementation (execution of approved proposals)

It is advisable that CEO and his team should handle all the functions of management, and the function of control should be under Board of directors. If any firm wants the quality of all four functions mentioned above, then separation is a must, so that the dual responsibility of CEO and chairman would be handled fairly. But if in unavoidable situation to combine the role of chairman and MD/CEO, then the board comprising non executive directors must be very strong.

2. Active Role of Institutional Investors

In the reforming practices of corporate governance, to strengthen the hands of institutional investors will contribute effectively. As if we talk about small investors or individual investors with small stake, they cannot play more active role because of 'free rider' problem. But the institutional investors can contribute highly towards improvement in corporate governance, as they have higher stake, 'Michel Porter' says– "Seek long term owners and give them a direct voice in governance a smaller number of long term or nearly permanent owners, thus creating a hybrid structure of 'Privately held' and publicly traded companies".

In this context it must be realized that financial Institutions must play a more active role than they do. Because of lack of incentives within the FIS, they don't show their effectiveness, there is a need to first improve their own governance and then turn up in better institutional investors.

3. Expand the Role of Non-executive Directions

To improve the quality of corporate governance, the role of non-executive directors must be enlarged because non executive directors can provide rich experience and good objectivity in monitoring corporate behavior.

CII (confederation of Indian Industry) has recommended code of corporate governance which are related with non- executive directors like —

- Non-executive directors should occupy at least 30% of the board seats.
- There must be a limit to the number of board on which a person can serve, CII has given the number is 10.
- An audit committee, having at least three non- executive directors must be set up and given access to all the information.
- The degree of accountability must be higher than at present.
- All the non-executive directors must be compensated well for their time and efforts.

4. Proper and Timely Information to the Board

It must be ensured that the Board is information-wise well-equipped. The board of directors should get full information about long-term plans, budgets, competitive developments, quarterly results etc. If the entire information about each and every corporate affair is easily accessible to BOD's, it would be quite easier for them to exercise the oversight functions.

5. Size of the Board

There is also kind of confession regarding the size of the board. 'Lipton and Loesch 'have done some excellent research work and provided the result with optimum size of the board is 10-12. If board is very long, it would be less effective as the main problem of co-ordination would occur, ordinarily the board should comprise of seven members. More over if we want competent, involved, accountable and well paid directions we have to limit the size of the board.

6. Improve Accounting and Reporting Practices

Accounting reports are the important means of information for the shareholders, creditors and investors of any company. We see in India, after the involvement of SEBI in corporate governance some improvement in corporate accounting and reporting practices has been seen, but still informed observer believe several reforms, improvement are required like –

(*a*) **Business line reporting–** Business line reporting says that the financiers should get integrated information about the profitability of different diversions of a single company. So it should be provided by the companies in line with the practice in developed capital market.

(*b*) **Group accounting–** The International accounting standards classify investor companies in three categories.

- Subsidiary companies
- Jointly controlled companies
- Associate companies

Therefore it is required that firms prescribe different accounting reporting treatments for these investments to reflect their financial implications.

But in India, at present we have just one accounting standard (AS-13) which classify investment in short term and long term and value them at fair market value. So Now Indian accounting practice should also follow these practices.

(*c*) **Tax effect accounting–**It eliminates the effects of timing differences in tax liability while arriving at reported earnings. As in India we find companies account for taxes as and when they are payable so it is difficult to calculate reported earnings.

(*d*) **Earning per share reporting–**EPS is a very commonly used term in stock market analysis but in Indian market there are no accounting standards prescribed for compiling EPS, no uniformity in the ways EPS is computed. But as we know that the practical significance of EPS is great, it is essential to formulate sound standards to calculate and report EPS in India.

Apart from the ways of reforming corporate governance there are some other ways like enhance contestability, link managerial compensation to performance, introduce the cumulative voting system also help management and Govt. to professionalize corporate governance practices. We are seeing some development in corporate governance.

According to 'Jayanth R. Varma'– "The past few years have witnessed a silent revolution in Indian corporate governance where managements have woken to the power of minority shareholders who vote with their wallets. They are adopting more healthy practices. These tendencies would be strengthened by deregulation, disintermediation, globalization, and tax reforms".

The confederation of Indian Industries (CII) Code–

The CII has suggested a code for its members. The main contents are like

- The role of non-executive directors should be expanded.
- Proper information about companies plans, budgets, Foreign-exchange

- exposure, managerial remuneration should be provided to the board.
- More information has to be disclosed to shareholders.

The SEBI Code –

The essence of the SEBI code which is based on the recommendations of the Kumar Mangalam Birla committee is as follows –

- Board meeting shall be held at least quarterly.
- At least 50% of the board shall comprise of non-executive directors and at least one third of the board shall comprise of independent directors.
- One section related to corporate governance should be there in annual report.
- Details of new appointment as directors shall be provided to the shareholders.
  - The auditors of the company should give a certificate regarding compliance on corporate governance.
  - The remuneration paid to all directors shall be disclosed in the annual report.
  - An audit committee of at least three non- executive directors shall be set up, the majority of them being independent.
  - It shall meet thrice a year.

9.7 HOW TO ACHIEVE GOOD CORPORATE GOVERNANCE

An Overall View

In the new millennium, the stake for corporate, wrong-doers has been raised dramatically. Big corporate accounting scandals like Enron, Tyco and world.com have shown the failure of financial accounting system, Corruption and weak corporate governance.

Most of the organizations have been found unable to keep pace with the complexity of this modern IT era. The structural factors contributing to this accounting crisis are like lack of financial transparency, fragmented business process, complex accounting practices hold down the visibility of internal and external stakeholders and company's financial health.

As the corporations are realizing the role of good corporate governance in the success of their business, they have started taking steps in improving the imbalance.

According to a recent information week survey reflect 70% of the companies are using technology tools to get accuracy in financial and accounting matters. But this much is not enough; they have to build a culture of integrity and responsibility among employees, monitor performance, proper communication.

With investors, enforcement of strict code of conduct to control so that the accounting scandals like Enron would not take birth.

The recent research findings conducted by Mc-Kinsey assure that all kinds of investors around the globe will pay a premium for share in the companies where standards of corporate governance would be high.

In-fact Indian companies also have a golden opportunity to become first movers and market leaders by investing in corporate integrity and regaining the trust of investors.

'ANAO' (The Australia's national audit office) suggests five key operating principles that demonstrate different dimensions of corporate governance which are —

1. **Leadership**–The basic fundamentals of effective corporate governance are leadership and direction. The CEO, M.D. other executive and non-executive director with good leadership styles, brilliant communication skills provide set of governance principles, balance and check the correct operations which are required by corporate governance.
2. **Management Environment**–Placing the principles to suggest the working is the basic function of management environment. The main focus is on to establish structures to support the achievements of corporate objectives which include -
   - Sound business planning and setting clear objectives.
   - Yardsticks for performance measures, evaluating performance with appropriate feed back.
   - Clear cut division of work and responsibilities.
   - Establish an ethical frame work.
   - Ensure right decision about the work force (right person for right job)
3. **Risk management**–Here risk management is not simply managing the risks which could present hindrance in achieving business objectives, but it includes some other diverse activities such as professional development, review of operating performance, the effective use of IT, adhering to appropriate delegations and disaster recovery plans.
4. **Monitoring**–Monitoring the quality of systems, from time to time is necessary to ensure that the systems, plans and procedures are operating effectively. With the help of proper and timely monitoring you can identify best practices, also you can defect the areas where improvement can be made.

   For this purpose the structure may have audit committees, internal audit units, system Appraisal and control self assessment.
5. **Accountability**– How much Accountable the working system is can be measured by effective internal and external reporting on conformance and performance against the set objectives.

   The key document providing the reporting framework is the corporate plan.

   The system prepares an accountability frame work which holds key accountability in areas like planning, staff management, budget management, reporting and corporate governance.

SUMMARY

Corporate governance is a way of life that necessitates taking into account the stake holder's interests in every sphere of business decision. Since 1990's, the concept of corporate governance has been gaining momentum. These are so many causes behind the origin of corporate governance. SEBI plays an important role in implementing corporate governance's practices. With the help of developed dimension of corporate governance like leadership, management environment, risk mgmt, monitoring and accountability etc, good corporate governance can be achieved.

QUESTIONS

1. What do you mean by corporate governance? Explain its historical background.
2. Discuss about the factors behind the origin of corporate governance.
3. Explain in detail about corporate governance in India for public sector as well as private sector.
4. Write an essay on How to achieve good corporate governance.

Part V

Ethics in Different Management Practice

Chapter 10

Ethics in Marketing

- *Introduction*
- *Common Unethical Practices*
- *Factors behind Ethical Practices*
- *Marketing Ethics–Important Issues*
- *Summary*

10.1 INTRODUCTION

Marketing is the task of creating, promoting and delivering goods and services to consumers and businesses. According to American Marketing Association "Marketing is the process of planning and executing the conception, pricing, promotion and distribution of ideas, goods and services to create exchanges that satisfy individual and organizational goods".

Or

Marketing is a societal process by which individuals group structure procure that they need or want freely exchanging goods and services value of it.

A no. of distinct functions comes under it like –

- Product development
- Distribution
- Pricing
- Promotion
- Sales

Now the question arises why should marketers worry about ethics? What role do the moral values play in an economic system? Is it the need of the hour to be ethical while marketing? Is it the competitive pressure/legal laws which force them to consider ethics in marketing or they have realized that in the changing climate of consumerism, they have to adopt ethical view to understand and meet the need of 21st Century customers.

Ethics in marketing is not all together a different concept or it is not performing marketing with a different concept/style but simply–

"It is the function and process of marketing keeping to the standard norms of it and achieving the ends through a sound means".

As we know that the focal point of ethics is 'normative' ('what ought' to be) rather than 'what is'. Though the ideal situations may vary from group to group and from time to time. Therefore, the marketers who wish to avoid criticism from competitors, customers, Govt., other stake holders must follow some ethics.

10.2 COMMON UNETHICAL PRACTICES

We will see these practices under 4 P's of mktg. mix–

Product	*Price*	*Place*	*Promotion*
Quality promotion	List price	Channels	Sales
Features	Discount	Locations	Advertising
Warranty	Credit terms	Inventory	Public relation
Brand name Marketing	Payment-period	transportation.	Direct
Size			
Packaging			
Design			

Therefore the common unethical practices are:

- Duplication of original brands.
- Inadequacy and insufficiency in warranty offering time and service.
- Not producing quality product.
- Question mark on products safety.
- Unauthorized manufacturing of hazardous products.
- Production of non- bio-degenerate plastic products which causes environmental pollution.
- Discrimination in pricing.
- Differentiation in pricing
- Excessive mark up prices.
- Misleading and deceptive advertisement.
- False promises.
- Lower the dignity of women.
- No fairness, transparency in relations with suppliers and retailers.
- Artificial scarcity.

This is an established fact that the right action is the one which produces the good results for the most people in specific situation. This can be a useful guide to develop and form marketing ethics.

10.3 FACTORS BEHIND ETHICAL PRACTICES

If the marketers want to run their business successfully in the long term, they must behave ethically; there are some crucial and pragmatic reasons which give backing to the application of ethical standards in marketing area like.

1. To Collect the Power by Society

Society gives the power to marketers, which they earn by their own efforts and influence so they should utilize their power in socially responsible and acceptable manner, other wise they might lose it.

2. Good will of the Organization

Now-a-day image, goodwill, reputations is big asset for any organization. As marketing executives represent whole organization and on the basis of contacts with them, society builds up the image of such company so they should be highly ethical and carry out the business in a dignified manner.

3. Government Regulations

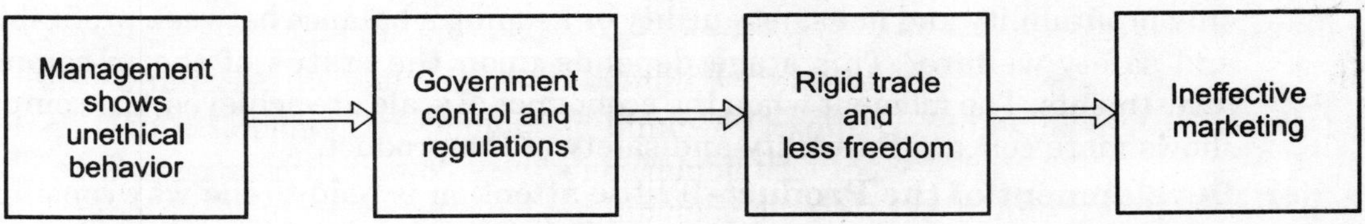

Therefore to avoid more government regulations they should become self regulatory by living up to the ethical mark up.

4. Build up Transparency

As unethical practices like misleading ads, low quality products, misleading package labels etc. are spreading rapidly, buyers become more suspicious while buying, therefore the big marketers and business leaders must take them into confidence by keeping high levels of transparency, convince the public that they are aware of their social responsibility and they will fulfill it because without society business cannot survive.

As it is absolutely clear from the above discussion that ethical behavior shown by the marketers is the need of the hour, still unethical practice are seen here and there and again there are some weighted reasons such as —

(*a*) People used to consider ethics and profits to be inconsistent and to some extent contradictory to each other. Though this concept is losing its effectiveness in 21st century scenario but still there is quite often little likelihood of immediate economic return to be more ethical than your competitor.

All business men are bound to follow certain laws which we say the smallest part of ethics, now if we decide to be more ethical in the market than others whether we are going to get profit or loss?

(*b*) The existing environment in particular industry firms may sometimes be dominant and influence the executives to behave in that particular prevailing practice.

(*c*) Acute competition–To cope with acute competition in the market and survive, marketers may practice unethical marketing.

10.4 MARKETING ETHICS-IMPORTANT ISSUES

Marketing ethics can be best understood in the light of its all marketing mix-product, price, place, promotion and people.

1. Ethical Product

Product is the first and fore-most important element of marketing mix. A product is any thing that can be offered to a market to satisfy need or want. The producers know more about the product than the buyer, so he should be extra careful as not to break the trust of the buyer. Chonko (1995) has given some conditions which should be considered while product development–

(*a*) **Initiation of the idea** – Who's creativity, is involved behind the idea to develop the product?

(*b*) **Planning and Screening of Product Design**–which criteria the firm follows—only profitability and not safety utility or keeping a balance between profitability and safety-welfare? This stage depends upon the status of the in-company investments. The moment when the economics of scale are achieved, the company shows more concern for utility and safety of the product.

(*c*) **Development of the Product**–If little attention is paid to the way consumers would actually use the products, the marketers must be ready to bear the consequences of failure of the product so the crux of marketing ethics says that extra precautions are required in product development and evaluation.

(*d*) **Marketing Strategy**–Which kind of marketing strategy should be adopted? How much strong is the product to face the competition?

Are extra efforts needed in marketing strategy to compensate some of its weak points? Or do you think you should be honest about its weak points?

As the very success of any product depends upon its marketing strategy so it is required to answer all the above questions before adopting any one.

(*e*) **Introducing the Product in the Market**–Should the company go for test marketing? What should be the sample size then? Should the company be transparent about its policies and strategies? Are they aware of the risks?

(*f*) **Decline Stage**–How the company should react in product decline stage? Should they go for some fair treatment try to over come with decline stage? Do the companies follow pushing strategy to push the product by devious means, once a letter product is available in the market?

2. Ethics in Pricing

Price is a critical element of Marketing mix which produces revenue. It communicates to the market the company's intended value positioning of its product or brand.

A firm must set a price for the first time when it develops a new product or when it introduces its regular product into new distribution channel. Companies generally do not go for a single price rather a price structure that has some variations according to purchase timing, order levels, geographical demands, market segment requirement like –

- Price Discounts
- Discriminatory Pricing
- Geographical Pricing

At this stage ethics comes into the picture. Here four major areas are most common in which unethical practices in pricing may occur –

(*a*) **Price Discrimination**–It occurs when a company sells a product/service at two or more prices that do not reflect a proportional differences in costs but it becomes illegal when seller offers different price terms to different people within the same group.

(*b*) **Predatory Pricing**–Selling below the cost when just having the intention to destroy competition.

(*c*) **Deceptive Pricing**–Deceive the customers to show them the wrong picture about the prices either by –

  (*a*) Low price offer

  (*b*) Inflated price

(*d*) **Price Fixation**– Prices are fixed at certain levels by firms either by–

- Horizontal price fixing – To fix the prices at artificially high levels.
- Vertical price fixing – Price fixing agreements between manufacturers and retailers or between manufactures and distributions. It says that product will be sold at the manufacturer's suggested price and will not be discounted by the retailer or wholesaler.

Here the concept of distributive justice given by (John Rawl's) can be applied as we say if unique universal pricing is established, then it would be against the distributive justice. On the other hand if a favourable price is providing towards the weaker section, though it would be a sort of discrimination but this would provide a desired justice to the weaker segment of society and this would be any where consider as ethical!

3. Ethical Promotion

Promotion plays an important role in marketing of any product/Service. It would come up with perfect outcomes only if the perfect means would have been adopted. Promotional mix consist of sales promotion, advertising, sales force, public relation, direct mail etc. Promotional claims must be of such type that the reality of the company and its standard must match.

Symmetry of information between the buyer and seller is an essential prerequisite for the ethicality of market system.

Unethical promotions are those where the company's offer varies significantly from its claims.

(a) Ethical issues in Advertising– Advertising is multi dimensional. It is a form of mass communication, a powerful marketing tool, a component of the economic system, a social institution, an art form, an instrument of business management, a field of employment and a profession or Advertising can be defined as any paid form of non-personal presentation of ideas, goods and services by an identified sponsor.

As earlier mentioned, Ethics is a choice between right and wrong, good or bad. It is governed by a set of principles of moralities at a given time, at a given place. Ethics is related to group behavior in ultimate analysis.

Advertising too has ethical values. Advertising communication is a mixed form of arts and facts. In order to be customer oriented an advertisement will have to be truthful and ethical. It should not mislead the consumers. If so happens the credibility is lost. Advertisement's truth is to be judged and viewed from the consumer's point of view, not in the narrow legalistic frame work. As we can say that in advertisement filed, it is very difficult to establish a clear line of demarcation between what is true and what is untrue.

Advertisement is judged by its impact, by its acceptance, by the consumers, what it promises to provide must be actually there in the performance of products.

As advertising is a social process, it must honor time tested norms of social behavior and should not affront our moral sense.

Advertising play two important functions:

Economic functions ⇒ Social functions

Economic Functions

The very basic function of all the advertisements is to promote any product/service by its unique strategies. So the advertisement agencies must accomplish all the ad's with: communicating properly and effectively

- Communicating to right people
- Communicating right message
- Put across thru brilliant and persuasive language
- Not only marketing the products but introducing and spreading corporate ethos and corporate philosophy.

Social Functions

Advertising must reflect the cultural values of that society as ads has affected not only the core cultural values but successful advertisement is consistent with society cultural values.

It can transfer some cultural values of one society to another at a given point of time.

4. Ethics in Channel

How to place your products and services cannot be overlooked because until and unless the product is well placed, the desired out come not be received.

To reach a target market, the marketer used three kinds of marketing channels–

(a) Communication Channels – Deliver and receive messages from target buyers and these include newspapers, magazines, radio, T.V. etc.

(b) Distribution Channels – These are used to sell or deliver product services to the buyers or users. They include distribution, wholesalers, retailers and agents.

(c) Service Channels – These are used to carry out transaction with potential buyers like banks, insurance, transportation companies etc.

Marketers clearly face a design problem in choosing the best mix of communication, distribution and the service channels for their offerings and here the scope of unethical practices may occur. Channel decisions taken by companies are very much influenced by companies' systematic and unsystematic factors. Once any one supplier, wholesaler start unethical practice, it would substantially reduce competition. Though it is hard to identify the unethical distribution strategies but when unethical means of expansion becomes the rule of the day it evaporates competition.

Conclusion

"Marketing ethics is a sub-set of business ethics and examines the moral issues relating to marketing decisions made by organizations. Although its roots can be traced back to the 1960s, marketing age is believed to have come of age only in 1990s, thanks to extensive research on the subject carried out in the decade before. (Murphy, 111). Several topics make up the fabrics of marketing ethics such as product quality, safety and liability, fairness in pricing, honesty in advertising and selling, privacy in internet database and marketing. According to Kotler, in recent years people have started questioning the value of marketing concept, when the world is faced with environmental degradation, resources shortages, hunger and poverty and neglected social services". [From the paper #052550: Marketing ethics]

SUMMARY

Marketing is a particular field, where we find the most common unethical practices seen in day to day dealings. The very common unethical practices are such as low quality products, discrimination in pricing, misleading advertisements, artificial scarcity, false promises regarding product and services etc. for long term survival, good will in the market and some other factors, we find ethics should be involved in marketing practices in each and every part like ethical product, ethics in pricing, ethical promotion and ethical channel of distribution.

QUESTIONS

1. Some marketers assume that marketing and ethics can not be combined. Explain your views.
2. What do you mean by ethical product? How ethics is involved in its development stages?
3. What are the basic major reasons for which marketers follow marketing ethics?
4. Throw light on Ethical advertising and ethical issues in promotional strategies.

CASE STUDY

Breast milk is a natural, safe and free human product. Breast feeding creates a strong material bond between mother and child and it is designed to protect the baby against a numbers of conditions such as pneumonia and diabetes.

Not only are these, but women who breastfeed themselves given greater protection against breast and ovarian cancers.

In this modern world, many women feel awkward in breast feeding and sometimes the medical staff do not have the time to provide adequate training to teach new mothers how to breastfeed.

Now, the infant formula is the obvious alternative. However this product is derived from cow's milk, which is not designed for humans. Though it can supplement the diet of a hungry baby, or help a working mother during the day, but it should not be marketed as an option that can replace breast milk entirely. The working mothers easily get convinced with the formula manufacturers, as the infant formula is much easier and more convenient to use. In developing nations, the area of breast feeding is very pathetic, sad and uneducated one. The big and powerful multinationals that control the world's infant formula market take all the advantages of the poor and uneducated in order to increase their own profits.

The world Health organization has a marketing code, endorsed by UNICFF and the UNHCR, which bans all promotion of baby milk - both through advertising and indirectly, through health workers and midwives, but these powerful companies pay little more than lip service to it. As the data says in the developing world, one baby dies every 30 seconds from unsafe bottle-feeding.

These are some MNCS which enjoys almost 40% of the world-wide infant formula and try to capture more and more. For this different marketing practice they conduct. They send their representative to developing countries identified as 'knowledgeable medial personnel', who give free samples of formula to hospitals and health workers. The medical staff, health workers nurses, all these encourage the mothers using the infant formula by providing free samples and therefore discouraging breast feeding obviously for promoting their products, companies give some sort of gifts and incentives to local health officials.

Other kind of promotion of their products is in the form of posters on the walls of clinics, some advertisements in national magazines etc. As the company's main aim is to encourage mother's to use the formula but they never provide adequate information about formula feeding. They do not teach these women about sterilizing the bottles they use, they provide no resources with which to do this. So the uneducated and unawared mothers use un-sterilized bottle and use dirty water mixed with formula which causes severe diarrhea and dehydration in the babies further which kill them.

Very soon, after the infants have become dependent on formula as their sole source of nutrition, and the mother's milk has dried up through lack of demand, the free samples stop coming. And now the only option left in front of mothers is to buy the packets with high prices. The majority of families cannot afford this. So either they go without food themselves and feed their babies or just over-dilute the powder to make it last longer. Again the babies will be suffering from malnourishment and often loss of lives.

These companies do not follow WHO Codes according to which they are required to put labels on formula products in the appropriate language. They actively promote the use of infant formula as opposed to breast milk and always try to make as healthy a profit as possible.

How for are these marketing practices ethical? Explain your view.

Chapter 11

Ethics in Finance

11.1 INTRODUCTION

Ethics and finance, a very new discovery. What role does ethics play in financial sector is not much discussed earlier. If we think deeply, we find that there is a close relationship between ethics and finance. Finance would be impossible without ethics. High finance is the particular area where most of the breakdowns of ethical norms occurred. The basic foundation of business is trust, as we place our money or our assets in the hands of other unknown people to carryout our business sometimes these unknown people come out as untrust-worthy like untrust agent or attorney. If we talk about finance, it's a very wide area full of complex activities, but broadly we find –

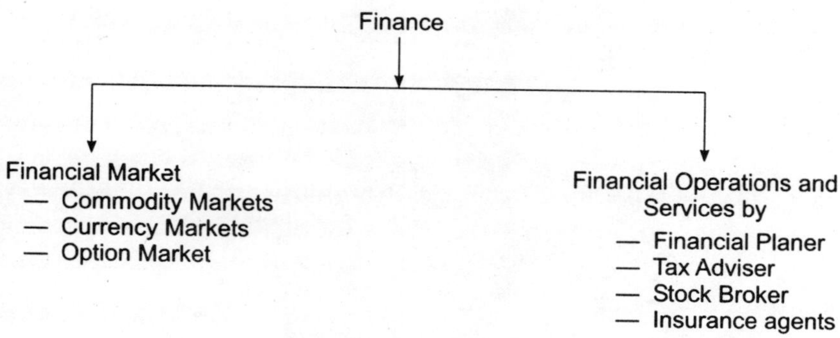

For smooth running of any economy, its financial activities must be ethical. Here we don't say that high return on investment or high interest rate etc. is not desirable. Good finance is the life blood of any organization.

As huge amount is involved in financial dealings people invest their money with financial institution, seeping their better life after the retirement, so there must be well developed and organized structure of ethics to ensure personal and organizational welfare.

Some Common unethical activities in Finance –

1. Unsuitability

Insurance agents, brokers and other sales-person cheat innocent investors by recommending unsuitable securities and financial products.

2. Deception

Deception is quite common unethical practice in India by strengthing the returns and minimizing the weaknesses and risk factors. Sales persons, agents, advisers deceive the public using the misleading statements like tax free or 0% interest etc. they make public unable to make rational choices among so many alternatives.

3. Inappropriate and Excessive Trading

This situation arises when the broker keeps an intention to generate commission rather than benefits to client in the standing of having control over the client's account. It's a kind of 'Churning' breach of a fiduciary duty.

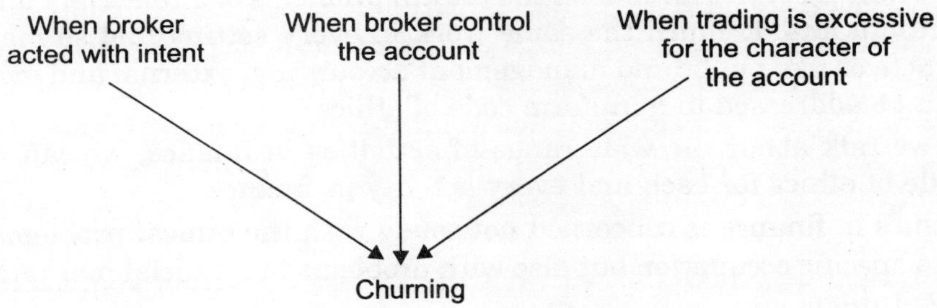

4. Fraud and Manipulation in Markets

As by law all the participants in the financial markets are same so fairness in our dealings is desired. Here the fairness is not meant by preventing losses rather it contributes to the efficiency. Here fraud means when a company fails to report proper information and manipulation of buying and selling of securities for the purpose of creating misleading impression about price to misguide the investors to buy or sell the securities.

The important information lays in the hands of issuing firms so the investors whether buyer/seller are vulnerable to fraud and manipulation.

They have to rely on the information available to them which is hard to verify.

5. Unequal Bargaining Power

It's a quite common unfair practice along with unequal information in the financial market. The principle of equal bargaining power says that all the parties have relatively equal bargaining power.

6. Insider Trading

The act of buying or selling a company's stock on the basis of 'inside' information about the company is called as 'insider trading'. Insider trading is illegal as well as unethical the information which is confidential and not available to the general public out side the company, have a significant impact on the price of the company's stock.

So the person who is practing insider trading in true manner steal this information and enjoys the unfair advantages over the member of the general public.

A lot more unethical practices are prevalent in corporate finance. It is felt by so many ignorant and unaware people that ethical can not be involved in finance but in reality we say that finance would be impossible without ethics because the very act of placing our assets in the hands of other people requires immense trust.

Ethics in finance is about far more than trust. It is too difficult to define a complete account which is the need for ethics in finance in few words –

- First of all finance is not like medicine, law. Accounting is not a clearly identifiable occupation or profession. It involves highly technical body of knowledge financial experts engage in a much wider range of activities.
- Accounting ethics focuses on the ethical problems of a relatively uniform activity. Accountants do much the same work in every setting and so many accounting practices like public and management accounting, external and internal auditing can be addressed in a uniform code of ethics.
- If we talk about the wide range of activities in finance, we can not find single code of ethics for each and every activity in finance.
- Ethics in finance is concerned not solely with the ethical problems of individual in a specific occupation but also with problems in financial markets and financial institutions.

Chapter 12

Ethics in Human Resource Management

- ***Introduction***
- ***Ethics in Job Design***
- ***Ethics in Human Resource Planning***
- ***Ethics in Recruitment and Selection***
- ***Ethics in Training and Development***
- ***Ethics in Career Development***
- ***Ethics in Performance Evaluation***
- ***Ethics in Wage and Salary Administration***
- ***Ethics in Layoffs***
- ***Ethical Guidelines***
- ***Summary***

12.1 INTRODUCTION

Human Resource Management is the process of acquiring, training, appraising and compensating employees and attending to their labor relations, health, safety and fairness concern. The policies and practices involved in carrying out the 'People' or HR aspects of a management position, including recruiting, screening, training, rewarding and appraising.

HR management activities like recruiting, hiring, training, compensation, apprising and developing employees is part of every manager job. It's also a separate 'staff' function and that the H.R. managers assist all managers in many important ways.

As far as HRM is concerned, what is ethical and what is unethical in general may not be easy to answer. As we know that ethics is the discipline dealing with what is good or bad and with moral duty and obligations. An organizations human resource policies and practices represent important forces for shaping employee behavior and attitudes. Thus there is a close linkage between HRM and ethics. Ethics in HRM can be defined as — Functioning and Performing HRM policies and practices with some standards norms, managing human resources so that mutual benefits can be achieved.

To understand the role of ethics in HRM, we go through the separate parts of human resource management and see how each one is related with ethical implications.

12.2 ETHICS IN JOB DESIGN

An understanding of job/work design can help executives to design and redesign job in such a way that it positively affects employee motivation. It includes work simplification, job rotation, job enlargement, job enrichment, job sharing, independent work teams, dejobbing and empowering the workforce.

(*i*) Job Rotation

Job rotation takes place when any employee suffers from over reutilization of his work. Then the employee is rotated to another job, at the same level that has similar skill requirements but sometimes we find some unethical issues like rotating the worker in the kinds of jobs where no innovative perspectives are present and the periodic shifts of workers may be the outcome of some conflicts among workers and employees who are involved in job design.

(*ii*) Work Simplification

It means simplifying the work of the employee, so they can understand it well and perform to full of their skills. The unethical issue has come in to the picture when work is over simplified that lead to boredom, more mistakes, less interests and tendering resignations.

(*iii*) Job Enlargement

Job enlargement is nothing but the horizontal expansion of jobs. This concept was introduced ground 40 years back. It increases the number and variety of tasks that an individual has to perform. Though motivational impacts are there of job enlargement, yet it may sometimes result in much more boring tasks.

(*iv*) Job Enrichment

Job enrichment is nothing but the vertical expansion of job. In fact to deal with the short comings of job enlargement, it has been introduced to deal with the shortcomings of enlargement.

In an enriched job, an employee would do the work with complete activities, more freedom and increased responsibility. The only thing which should be handled carefully is to take care while selecting the employee whose job should be enriched.

(*v*) Job Sharing

Job sharing is simply the practice of having two or more people split a 40 hour week job. So people find it as an opportunity to get an experience of two heads. The unethical issue involve here is to intentionally involve two person to do single job who do not successfully coordinate.

(*vi*) Dejobbing

Dejobbing is the practice in this global environment which checks the companies from overstaffing to prepare committed employees. But it is more suitable for the competitive markets. It is not ethical to go for dejobbing if not required at all.

(*vii*) Empowerment

In this option employees go for requiring skills and additional knowledge to do the job in which they have their interest and aptitude.

12.3 ETHICS IN HUMAN RESOURCE PLANNING

Human resource planning is an interpreted approach to performing personnel function in order to have a sufficient supply of adequately developed and motivated people to perform the duties and tasks, required to meet organizational objectives and satisfy the individual needs and goals of the organizational members.

Thus the main objective behind HRP is to get workforce in the desired form of the organization. A successful human resource planner is the one who plans out for human resources in such a way that in future the firm will get adequately developed skilled people to carry out the activities and contribute in the firm's growth. So if we apply ethics in HRP what can be said is the main theme of utilitarian theory which suggest if out come of any event or activity is well it is ethical. Thus we can say that if the manager is able to re-plan for that kind of workforce who will be really required and proved out the best it is ethical. But, if not it comes out as unethical conduct of the HR planner.

12.4 ETHICS IN RECRUITMENT AND SELECTIONS

Recruitment is the process of searching for prospective employees and stimulating them to apply for job in an organization.

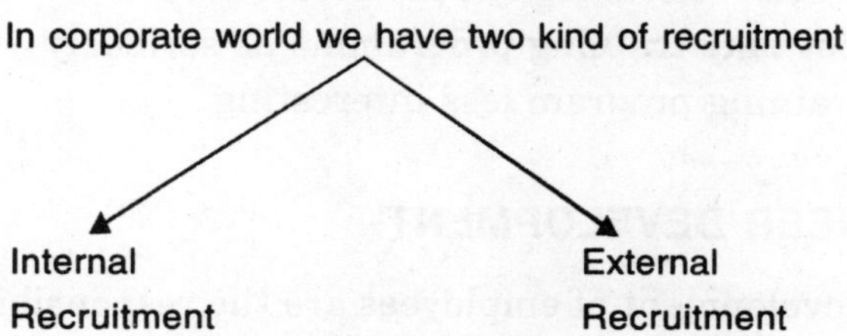

First any organization search for a suitable person for its requirement internally, so people say it is been ethical towards the employee, they would get good changes of their promotion if the company opts internal recruitment.

But as we know, now the world demands highly skilled and talented people. So suppose if the internal sources are not as skilled as required, the company should hunt for suitable candidates outside, if the company recruits internal candidates, even though they are not suitable to the job requirement. It would be unethical.

Though people say that an organization is more ethical if it goes for internal recruitment and further provides training and development to the employees, if required. But how far is it ethical to make compromises as far as skill and talent concern?

In any organization so many selection devices have been used like interviews written tests, performance simulation tests etc. There are also some practical ethical questions arise like.

(*a*) Sometimes the organizations select unsuitable employees due to pressure from top level, some internal politics etc. If it happens in selection process, it directly leads towards inefficiency and then has impact on organization growth and productivity.

(*b*) Selection of a candidate as he/she suits the job is ethical but when people make some adjustment in job specification according to the suitability of the candidate just because of any corrupt activity, it is called as unethical !

(*c*) The practice of taking more employee than the need is also a common unethical practice in selection procedure.

12.5 ETHICS IN TRAINING AND DEVELOPMENT

Competent employees don't remain competent forever competency, skills deteriorate and can become obsolete.

So organizations spend a good amount on training and development.

Training is an organized procedure by which people learn knowledge/skill for a definite purpose. It can be basic literacy, technical, interpersonal and problem solving. It improves the skills and increases employee's self-efficacy.

Some unethical practices make training sometimes ineffective like –

- When trainers are less qualified and less interested in providing training.
- Trainees have been selected not as per needs, but based in favoritism and nepotism.
- Trainees do not take training programme as seriously as they should.
- Making the training program less interesting.

12.6 ETHICS IN CAREER DEVELOPMENT

Career planning and development of employees are the responsibility of employee as well as the management. Though, it is increasingly being done by individual employee rather than by the management. As far as organization's responsibilities concern the managers should create growth opportunities, offer financial assistance, communicate organization's goal and future strategies etc.

From employee side they should be aware of themselves, manage the reputation, build and maintain network contacts and keep the options open.

So from any side whosoever is shrinking their responsibilities towards themselves or towards other party is deemed as unethical.

12.7 ETHICS IN PERFORMANCE EVALUATION

Performance evolution is needed for so many purposes compensation, performance feedback, training promotion and Research etc.

The main objective of performance evaluation is to access accurately an individual's performance contribution as a basis for making reward allocation decisions. As it is always beneficial to the organization as well as to the employee but sometimes people do not take performance evaluation, as it should be. They conduct some activities related with evaluation just for formality. This happens mostly in public sector undertakings where people are very rigid for change, not give much importance for self-development as well as organization's development.

12.8 ETHICS IN WAGES AND SALARY ADMINISTRATION

It is also a very important part of any company's human resource practices. The wages policies before 1991 were based on socialistic patterns like —

Minimization of the gap between the highest and the lowest wage, payment of equal ways to all the employees doing the same job irrespective of their job performance, reduction in wage/salary inequalities. But a no. of questions arise regarding the wage and salary administrations ethical issues.

Some queries are like — Is it fair to give equal payment to the employees one who does the least and other who makes the highest contribution to the job?

How for it is ethical to give bonus the rate of 8.33% of the annual basic pay of the employee if company is under losses?

Though, in this 21st Century there are some industries which have already started paying, the employees, based on their contribution and very soon this concept would be implemented in other industries in the 21st century.

12.9 ETHICS IN LAYOFFS

Layoff is a kind of practice which means discharging the unneeded workers temporarily. Now a day's organizations in every segment of business industry, govt. or education are downsizing. Is it ethical? It's difficult to answer, but in any case we can say that it is not necessarily desperate move on the part of failing and non- profit making company.

12.10 ETHICAL GUIDELINES

As we have seen ethics is involved in each and every corner of HRM. Thus here in the following section some guidelines have been provided to HR professional by which they would be able to handle it in much better ways.

(*A*) Ethical Leadership

Human resource professional should exhibit individual leadership as a role model for maintaining the highest standard of ethical conduct. The intention behind ethical leadership is like –

- To earn individual respect.
- To earn our credibility with those whom we serve.
- To set example and standard for others.

Some guidelines have been developed for the HR managers which would help them to exhibit Ethical leadership –

1. be ethical and act ethically in every sphere of professional interaction.
2. To check out individual and group actions regarding the ethical decisions are implemented in an ethical manner.
3. To for expert opinion and guidance if any doubt about the ethicality of any situation.
4. Generate more ethical leaders in organization by teaching and monitoring.

(*B*) Professional Responsibility

In today's scenario the important responsibility of HR professional is to add value to the organization which they serve and contribute to the ethical success of the organization. The purposes and aims behind developing professional responsibility are –

- To influence workplace and recruitment practices
- To assist the organizations in achieving their objectives and goals.
- To encourage professional decision making and responsibility.
- To build up credibility, respect and strategic importance for HR profession internal as well as external.

Guidelines

Some guidelines which make HR professional to discharge there professional responsibility –

1. Strive to achieve the highest levels of service, performance. and social responsibility.
2. Achieve and maintain the highest standards of ethical and professional behavior.
3. Practicing the appropriate use and appreciation of human beings as employees.
4. Comply with the law.
5. Consistency of work with the value of the profession should be maintained.
6. To influence decision making and results, advocate open debate well within the established forums.

(*C*) Fairness and Justice

The care ethical responsibility of HR professional is to promote and faster fairness and justice for all employees and their organizations. The basic intention behind that is to create and sustain an environment that encourages all individuals and the organization to reach their fullest potential in a positive and productive manner.

Guidelines

1. Treat people with respect, dignity and compassion to develop an environment which would be free from harassment, intimidation and discrimination.
2. Plan, develop, manage and advocate policies and procedure that foster fair consistent and equal treatment to all.
3. The organization's decision legal and ethical irrespective of personal interests must be supported.
4. Each individual has some uniqueness and intrinsic worth, so respect for it.
5. An inclusive approach in the organization should be followed which ensure that each and every one in the organization has an opportunity to develop the skills
6. If the organization deals in international businesses then sound management practices with full of responsibilities should be shown.

(*D*) Professional Development

As professional development is a non-ending continuous process. The professionals must strive to meet the highest standards of competence and commit to strong them the competencies. The basic purposes behind the development are –

(*a*) To broaden the understanding of how organization carry out the work.

(*b*) To expand and advance the knowledge about HRM to better understand how the organization function.

Guidelines

Some guidelines for HR professionals for their professional development:

1. Commitment for continuous learning and skill development.
2. Try to pursue formal academic opportunities.
3. Contribute to the evolution of the profession and the growth of individuals through research and development teaching.

(*E*) Conflicts of Interest

The HR professionals must maintain a high level of trust with their stake holder. They should protect the professional integrity and the interest of all the stakeholders. They should not engage in the kind of activities which create potential conflict of interests. This principle has been developed with the intention to avoid conflicts which may appear with any of the provisions of this code of ethical and professional standards in HRM.

Guidelines

1. Make a list of priority obligations to identity conflicts of interest.
2. Advocate the use of published policies on conflicts of interests within the organization.
3. Never-ever indulge in giving or seeking preferential treatment in human resources processes.
4. Using the power of the position for personal material or financial gain is unethical.

(*F*) Use of Information

It is the basic duty of HR professionals to ensure that there is a flow of truthful communication and informed decision making in the organization where they serve. They should maximize the open exchange of information by this they would be able to build trust among all organizations constituents and it would reduce the worries about inaccurate and inappropriate information among the members of the organization.

Guidelines

1. Acquire and provide information through ethical and responsible means.
2. Maintain up to date as well as accurate HR information.
3. Proper investigation about the accuracy and source of information before it is to be used in decisions.
4. Take care and safeguard measures for restricted or confidential information.
5. Take proper steps to ensure the accuracy and competence of all communicated information about HR Policies.
6. Take proper steps to make it sure that the above information is used in HR related training.

SUMMARY

Human resource management is one of the important part of management function of any organization. Therefore there are various HRM practices like training and development, hiring and firing, wage and administration etc. that exert a powerful influence on ethical practices. There are some specific guidelines to HR professional by which they can effectively conduct HR practices ethically.

QUESTIONS

1. Should Ethics be involved in various HRM policies? Why?

2. Explain the role of ethics in Training and development.

3. "As HRM system vary from country to country, so it is difficult for global companies to establish ethical system connected to HRM system" comment on it.

4. Discuss the ethical guidelines to help HR professionals in dealing with ethical issues of HRM.

Chapter 13

Ethics in Information Technology

- **Introduction**
- **Computer Ethics**
- **Ethical Issues**
- **Preventing Crimes and Ethical Dimension**

13.1 INTRODUCTION

Information technology refers to the creation, gathering, processing, storage and delivery of information and the processes and devices that make all this possible. The works that are handled using IT continue to increase almost on a daily basis. No matter what field of study you are in, or where you are employed, you'll be sure to find IT at work.

Information technology is new to the world is which the clear legal environment is not developed till now, so getting benefits and competitive advantage, by using IT, can not be surely ethical/legal as ethics (earlier mentioned) is a choice between right and wrong, true or false. So when we talk about Ethics and IT many new issues and dimensions are in front of us.

IT is a particular field which has no geographical boundaries but application and usages of IT may affect differently in different culture and different environment.

The aspects which are purely acceptable in one culture might be unethical in another. As computers do not know borders, computer network have a truly global character so when we talk about computer ethics, we are talking about emerging global ethics.

13.2 COMPUTER ETHICS

Computer ethics was founded by NIT professor Norbert Wiener in early 1940's during world-war two, when he was helping to develop an aircraft cannon capable of shooting down fast warplanes. He along with some colleagues created a new branch of science called as "Cybernetics"– the science of information feed back system. By combining cybernetics with digital computers, he fore-saw revolutionary social and ethical consequences. In his book cybernetics:

Control and communications in the animal and the machine, he said –

"It has long been clear to me that the modern ultra rapid computing machine was in principle".

Technology Ethics

Technology ethics is now very new and interesting subject. Some few related terms which become part of technology ethics are like –

1. Think ethically about human biotechnology.
2. Taking responsibility for E-Wastage like environmental damage from computer and other electronic waste.
3. With the help of new technologies employers must check whether employees are wasting time at recreational web sites or sending unprofessional e-mails.
4. The use of cloning– "just because we can, should we?" As "If we can, we will is a dangerous motto".
5. Cyber smut– from blocking software to legislation, strategies address children's access to objectionable material on the internet.
6. Sometimes the invasions of privacy occurs using internet services.
7. Some ethical issues raised by the use of E-mail about how we treat one another and how we work. The issue of e-mail ownership has other ethical ramifications that might go under the headings of attribution. Who is the true author of a message and how should he or she be acknowledged?

"An ideal central nervous system to an apparatus for automatic control and that its input and output need not be in the form of numbers or diagram but might very well be, respectively, the readings of artificial sense organs, such as photoelectric cells and the performance of motors or solenoids. We are ready in a position to construct artificial machines of almost any degree of elaborateness of performance long before Nagasaki and the public awareness of the atomic bomb; it had occurred to me that we were here in the presence of another social potentiality of unfired of importance for good and for evil".

'Wiener expressed his view very clearly that the integration of computer technology into society would have remarkable impact.

Computer revolution would be multifaceted on going process of decades and would radically change everything. But the actual momentum the new area of applied ethics had received around mid 1960's from 1940's to 1960 this complex area was remained unexplored and undeveloped and ignored.

By the mid 1970's new privacy laws and computer crime laws had been enacted in America and in Europe, Again in 1970's. 'Walter Maner' felt to innovate a separate branch of applied ethics 'computer ethics' which he defined as computer ethics is the branch of applied ethics which studies ethical problems- "aggravated, transformed or created by computer technology."

James Moor, in one of his classic essay described computer ethics like – "A typical problem in compute ethics arises because there is a policy vacuum about how computer technology should be used. Computers provide us with new capabilities and these in turn give us new choices for action. Often, either no policies for conduct in these situations exist or existing policies seem inadequate.

A central task of computer ethics is to determine what we should do in such cases, *i.e.* to formulate policies to guide our actions of course; some ethical situations confront us as individuals and some as a society. Computer ethics includes consideration of both personal and social policies for the ethical use of computer technology.

In Moor's view computer ethics include –

1. Identification of computer generated policy vacuums.
2. Clarification of conceptual Muddles.
3. Formulation of policies for the use of computer technology.
4. Ethical justification of such policies.

13.3 ETHICAL ISSUES

There are various ethical issues involved in information technology. In 1986 'Masovi' had categorized the ethical issues in four groups like.

(*A*) Accessibility

It involves the right of accessing the required information as well as the true payment of charges to access the information.

(*B*) Privacy

It deals with the degree of privacy and dissemination of information about individual.

(*C*) Property

It talks about ownership and value of information.

(*D*) Accuracy

The information which is viable and being accessed is now much more accurate and authenticate.

Other ethical issues may arise by the use of IT in following areas –

- Health
- Crime
- Employment
- Working conditions
- Individuality

Information systems are very complex and have many components so as very vulnerable to many hazards. Some threats to information systems are like –

- Computer abuses
- Computer crimes

- Loss
- Theft of equipment
- Theft of data
- Equipment malfunctions
- Environment hazards (flood, power failure, storms, earthquake and fires)
- Destruction from viruses.
- Errors in handling and usages of data.

As the percentage of users of IT is increasing at the rapid pace same as the no. of crimes are increasing. Computer crimes like unauthorized access and use of computers, destruction of alteration of data or software, embezzlement are spreading world widely.

At one side where people get benefits using computers and technologies, other sides is having threats with all these unethical practices.

13.4 PREVENTING CRIMES AND ETHICAL DIMENSION

Now the time has come to apply efficient preventive measures to prevent computer crimes like –

1. Make separate the employee functions so that they won't be able to do any malpractice in other's work and so rotate workers from critical positions.
2. At the time of recruitment, fire trust worthy people, though difficult to be detected but it is the most national way to prevent crimes.
3. Proper restriction on system uses.
4. Surprise and frequent audits must be conducted to make people scared of doing crimes.
5. Proper protection of resources with pass words.
6. Timely monitoring the system like who logged on and off.

The computer ethics institute in Washington, DC, has proposed the following ten commandments of computer ethics –

1. Thou shalt not use computer to harm other people.
2. Thou shalt not interfere with other people's computer work.
3. Thou shalt not snoop around in other people's computer files.
4. Thou shalt not use a computer to steal.
5. Thou shalt not use a computer to bear false witness.
6. Thou shalt not copy or use proprietary software for which you have not paid.
7. Thou shalt not use other people's computer resources without authorization or proper compensation.
8. Thou shalt not use other people's intellectual output.
9. Thou shalt think about the social consequences of the program you are writing or the system you are designing.
10. Thou shalt always use a computer in ways that demonstrate considerations and respect for your fellow humans.

Part VI

Business and Society

Chapter 14

Environmental Ethics

- Introduction
- Meaning of Environmental Ethics
- Pollution
- The Facets of Environmental Ethics
- Environmental Protection in India
- Some Examples
- Summary

14.1 INTRODUCTION

An environment can be said as the totality of man's surroundings. It includes water, air and land and their interrelationship with human beings, other living creatures, plants, micro organisms and property.

The Environment is made up of two things –

Environment

National resources
- — Land
- — Air
- — Water
- — Fuels
- fauna and flora
- — Raw materials
- — Minerals

Man- made resources
- — People
- — natural
- — heritage
- — socio-economic
- — structure

14.2 ENVIRONMENTAL ETHICS—MEANING

How to keep a balance between business and environment has been a burning issue in this industrialization era. Due to rapid spreading of environmental consciousness, the traditional perception about a trade off between environmental quality and economic growth is also changing. Now people believe that these two concepts-economic growth and environmental quality are complementary.

Though the current focus on environment is not new. It has been an integral part of the Indian culture. More than three thousand years ago the need for conservation and sustainable use of natural resources has been expressed in Indian scriptures. Even before 1947, several environment legislation existed but the real developed framework came only after the UN conference on the Human Environment (Stockholm, 1972).

14.3 POLLUTION

Pollution has become the first enemy of mankind. It is not a new phenomenon. It is as old as civilization it self. Dr. Kurt Waldheim, the Secretary General of United Nations addressing a conference in 1972, observed that pollution of environment is a problem, "no nation, no continent, no hemisphere, no race, no system can handle alone. He further observed that "the quality of our atmosphere can be nothing else but the by-product of the behaviour of the nations".

Air Pollution

Air is the most essential necessity of human beings. 30 lbs of air is the minimum requirement every day of an average man.

The dry air has concentration of certain gases, which are naturally present in the atmosphere. So when this balance of natural composition of air is disturbed and have an adverse effect on man or environment can be called as air pollution. Pollutants may be generated by interaction among two or more primary pollutants or may be directly emitted into the atmosphere from the identifiable sources like — Solids, aerosol, metallic dust fluorides vehicular smoke, nitrogen compounds etc.

Adverse Affects

Air pollution adversely affects human beings, animals, vegetation or other materials for ex. When the air pollutant carbon monoxide is inhaled it displaces the oxygen in the blood and reduces the amount of oxygen carried to the body tissues. The gases impose an extra burden on the human being who is already suffering from anemia, or certain heart diseases or some blood pressure problems and overactive thyroid.

Similarly sulphur-oxide can cause temporary and permanent injury to the respiratory system. Air pollution has wide spread damage on plant life, materials and building. Pollution control program must consist of legal, institutional, scientific and technological efforts to avoid or mitigate such excesses in the environment. It can be done by devising new technologies of manufacture that minimize or reduce pollutants and by recycling materials and commodities through reprocessing and resource recovery.

Water Pollution

As we know that water is plentiful, but pure water is scarce, which has a critical importance to life and that it would be difficult to think of life on any planet with out it Apart from air pollution, water pollution is also very serious and dangerous.

According to central Board for prevention and control of water pollution, the fresh water that is so essential to our lives is only a small portion of the earth's total water supply; it is only about two percent of the total.

So water pollution can be defined as, " Such contamination of water or such alteration of the physical, chemical or biological properties of water or such discharge of any sewage or of trade effluent or of any other liquid, gaseous or solid substance into water.

John R. Hobum defined water pollution as "the addition to water of an excess of material (or heat) that is harmful to humans, animals or desirable aquatic life, or otherwise causes significant departures from the normal activities".

There are many sources of water pollution –

(*a*) Industrial effluent directly entering into a stream or through a municipal sewer or through a discharge on land meant for irrigation causes water pollution.

(*b*) Most of the community wastage is discharged into the water sources.

(*c*) The uses of fertilizers also sometimes become the source of water pollution, when unused nitrogenous fertilizer is drained out of soil into likes and rivers.

(*d*) Using pesticides in agriculture may also cause pollution due to rain water washing into stream.

(*e*) Air pollutions may also be the sources of water pollution.

(*f*) Ground water is being polluted due to dump trade or sewage effluent into under ground strata.

(*g*) The dumping and covering of vegetable materials in garbage result in their decomposition by percolating water into underlying ground water bodies from the articles.

It is very crucial to control water pollution. Though in India some govt. acts and laws have been established like the water (Prevention and control of pollution) Act, 1974. But until and unless effective measures are taken by either governments or by general public, it is difficult to get rid off it.

Earth Warming

Earth's atmosphere is warming continuously due to man-made activity and natural causes. Scientists deeply involved in the research to seek the answer as to who is more responsible for this changing climate and temperature of earth– Man or nature?

Undoubtedly we can say that there are some natural causes like sulphate droplets called 'aerosol' cast a lot by corrupting volcanoes that reflect the sunlight and cool the atmosphere changes in solar radiation.

But man made causes like disposal of toxic, waste, emission of waste industrial gases like CO_2, sulphate aerosol from industrial smoke, eroding of the earth's ozone layer acid rain.

Ozone Depletion

For over 50 years chloro-fluorocarbons (CFCs) were thoughts of as miracle substances. They are stable, non-flammable, low in toxicity and in expensive to produce. Over times CFC found to be used in refrigerator, solvent other chlorine containing compound methyl chloroform and carbon tetrachloride an industrial chemicals.

All these compound have atmospheric life time along enough to allow them to be transported by winds in the stratospheres.

Because they release chlorine/Bromine, when they break down they damage the protective ozone layer.

Noise Pollution

Noise is a part of human life and a natural product of human life and environment. So man has a relationship with noise from cradle to grave. To express our happy and sad moments of life we use noise. Sometimes we do silent compromise to take noise as a normal part of our life without realizing that some times it adversely affects our health.

Even noise pollution was not discussed in Stockholm conference (1971) at National and international level, it was exposed after scientific research about the most dangerous effects of noise on man's health.

Industrialization urbanization, created the most acute problem of our century - noise pollution. Population explosion further expanded the problem of noise pollution. As the population increase, there are massive increases in human activities in all spheres connected directly or indirectly with the human, beings. Commercialization, further added to the intensity and extent of the problem of noise pollution.

But the sad part is most of the people are unconscious of the immediate and ultimate ill effects of noise, so life simply goes on without any tangible protest from the public.

But there are a no. of effects of noise pollution on man. It may cause heart attack, may change a mark psychological state, hypertension/ulcers and damage one's hearing capacity.

Now here what exactly we mean by noise –

In the words of Harrell, "Noise is an unwanted sound which increases fatigue and under some industrial conditions it causes deafness".

According to Blum, "noise is a distracter and there fore, interfering with efficiency".

According to J. Tiffin, "Noise is a sound which is disagreeable for the individual and which disturbs the normal way of an individual".

The effects of noise can be broadly divided into two parts –

→ Psychological

→ Physiological

The undesired sound (noise) may cause annoyance. Prolonged chronic noise can also produce stomach ulcers. It may cause abortions and other congenital defects in unborn children.

Therefore, some of the conscious efforts can be made to control noise pollution –

1. **Administrative Efforts**
   Administration is the strong arm of the state which dominates in policy and planning of all the development programmes of the state. The administrative agencies play a quite important role in giving effect to any legal process and as much the commitment and sincerity level is high, more success in preventing the pollution.
2. **Judicial Efforts**
   Judicial efforts can also be proved very effective in dealing with noise pollution. Judiciary should exercise the discretion of judicial review in favour of administrative orders and must reflect its concern for environmental protection by providing effective remedies to persons who approach the court.
3. **Legislative Efforts**
   Legislative action is the most effective approach. As laws are the instruments of social changes, so as other bodies administrative and passed by legislature and operate within the limitation prescribed by law.
4. **Public Involvement**
   Any law or judicial activity will remain ineffective if public doesn't take active part and fully Cooperate with any programme towards securing pollution free environment.
5. **International Co-operation**
   As pollution is not restricted to one country or another country, it is spreading its roots universally. National action needs to be supplemented by international measures and co-operation. It can be achieved by exchange of appropriate technology, research programmes, legal and other methods.

   In the early, 1970s researchers began to investigate the effects of various chemicals on ozone layer, particularly CFCs, and other chlorine resources – Chlorine from swimming pools, industrial plants, sea salt — they do not reach to stratosphere, they rain out of the troposphere very quickly.

   In contract CFCs are very stable and do not resoling in the rain. Over times winds drive the CFCs into stratosphere. The CFCs are so strong that only exposure with UV rays breaks them down then CFC molecule resale chlorine atoms that can destroy over 1, 00,000 ozone molecules? Numerous research and experiments have shown that CFCs and other widely used chemicals produce roughly 85% of the chlorine in the stratosphere while natural sources contribute only 15%.

   For Example – Ozone hole over Antarctica that has occurred during the Antarctica spring since the early 1980s, and this hole is a large area of the stratosphere with extremely low amount of ozone.

In addition research has shown that ozone depletion occurs over the latitudes that include North America, Europe, Asia and much of Africa, South America. Thus ozone depletion is a global issue.

Reduction in ozone layer will lead to higher levels of UV rays reaching the earth surface. Laboratory studies suggest that UV rays cause skin cancer, some health problems, damage to crops and other materials and certain type of marine lives.

It is difficult to figure out the weight age of human activity impact on earth's climate basically earth's climate is affected like –

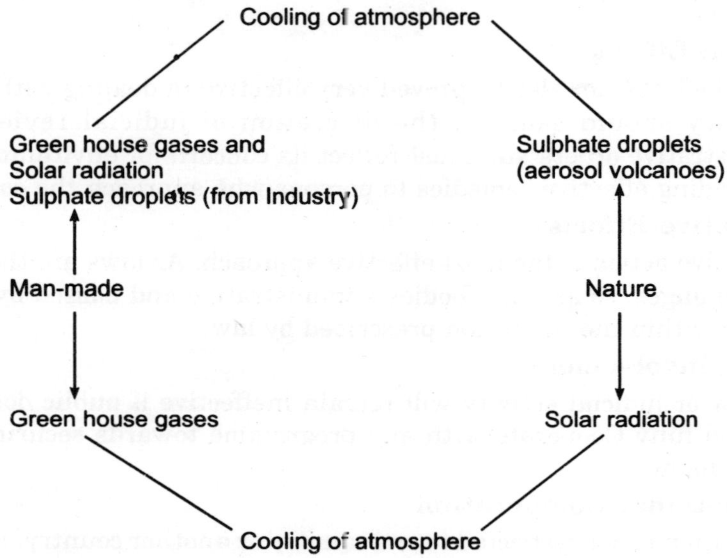

From the above diagram though it is obvious that warming and cooling of the atmosphere are affected by both (Natural and man made) factors but the human activity causes are more and more dangerous. So the researchers suggest that strict controlled actions should be taken by each and every nation.

Role of Ethics in Environmental Protection

Chakraborty (1995) says, "While commending Indian values in Environment protection as he sees them, many would not see the Indian past as kindly as he does. Western thinkers more often then not, look at environmental ethics as basically human centered and not nature controlled. The definitions of environmental and environmental pollution in Indian law are amenable to be used both as a human central and nature centered values".

As the magnitude of the problems of environmental pollution are increasing whose root causes sources are in industrial production. Seeing these threatening situations, people started thinking about environment ethics, which has now become an essential part of business ethics.

The concept of environment ethics is a recent discovery. It says understand the situation, identify the causes the disorder or imbalance occurred in environment, take preventive measures to eliminate it or else reduce it.

14.4 THE MAIN FACETS OF ENVIRONMENT ETHICS

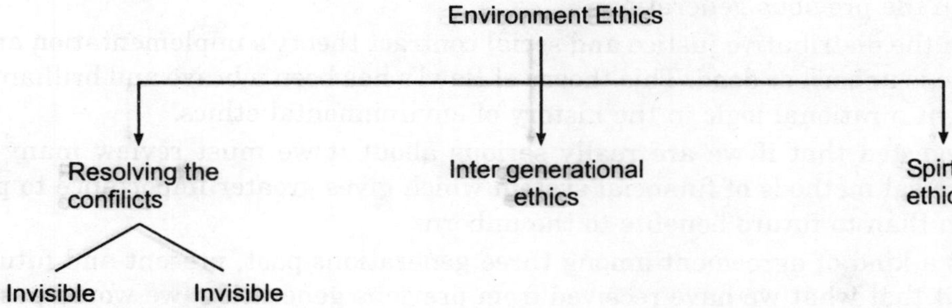

(*I*) Resolving the Conflicts

The origin of conflict of interest can be understood in two ways:

(*A*) Invisible Area

Conflicts of interest in invisible areas are due to development and operations of market systems. Industrialist says that if industry produces, smoke has to come out, pollution is unavoidable. If we take preventive and corrective measures we could reduce it a bit but someone else would destroy the environment if they do not.

If simply means that in the expansion, growth of no. of industries, multiple machines which produce million and million tons of products, industrialist are aware of themselves, they look after their own affairs, little information about others though similar business, similar industry but called as competitors. So they all are doing harm, destroy the environment and they jointly destroy the common environment. So this face of environment ethics says that if they unite, cooperate with each other, keep adequate information of the others and understand the basic concept which might be invisible that environment protection is for their mutual good, so it should be protected.

Though selfishness is inherent characteristics of any human being but this thing also could make them unite and cooperate with each other. Some institution should be invented in which each one is accountable for what he does, contributive efforts would make it work. Some union government laws can also be made, simultaneously some incentive schemes like subsidies, tax concessions to support for environmental protection.

(*B*) Visible Area

Another visible area is a direct consequence of the concept of rights that has taken root in India. It says that India's environmental problems arise from the deliberate actions of the state not because of market forces.

(*II*) Intergenerational Ethics

This is an important face of environment ethics. It deals with the activities of mankind which have direct consequences upon the lives of the future generations.

This concept has been given by Rawls (1971) who argues, "In a situation like this, distributive justice would require that one should pass on to posterity that one wants or inherits from the previous generations.

Though the distributive justice and social contract theory's implementation are with a person who is unborn or dead. This theory of Rawl's has been a brave and brilliant effort which brought a rational logic in the history of environmental ethics.

He suggested that if we are really serious about it we must review many of our project appraisal methods of financial system which gives greater importance to present consumption than to future benefits to the unborn.

So it is a kind of agreement among three generations-past, present and future. We must commit that what we have received from previous generation, we would pass on to the future generation.

(*III*) Spiritual Ethics

When Ethics extends its hands to reach animals, birds, plants and inanimate objects, this is some thing which we say spirituality in environmental ethics.

So ethics scope is not restricted to human centered but to be life centered, animal centered, rock centered.

"The new vision of deep ecology is consistent with perennial philosophy of spiritual traditions, another of Christian mystics of the Buddhists or of the American Indian traditions".

The ultimate of Environment Ethics-Capra and Pauli (1996)

In India we find that from ancient times Indian Philosophers thought of the environment. Indians had a scared respect for the environment from the time of 'Rig Veda', it had been involved in our culture to talk, think, respect about environment and its parts.

But the sad part of this picture is in this new century, due to much industrialization, materialistic attitudes, poverty, population explosion, unemployment etc. Indians are showing some different attitudes and treatment towards environment which is far away from the concept of spiritual ethics.

14.5 ENVIRONMENT PROTECTION IN INDIA

Environment protection in India is not new. Though the traditional concept and modern views are different but in our Indian scriptures this topic had been expressed three thousand years ago.

Indian government, politicians, entrepreneurs, businessmen all have now realized that the time has come to think seriously about this serious issue of environment pollution. They admit that environment is to be protected.

India's approach towards environment issue is changing, social workers, NGO's and government involvement in environmental concern are increasing.

To make our younger generations aware of environmental theories, laws, environment pollution, etc. its affects, harms etc., a subject in their course curriculum has been started at different stages.

Recently, In Maharashtra State Government has declared that from this session a new subject is to be launched on environment as a compulsory subject of 100 marks in SSC Board exams.

Due to government strict rules, regulations, timely monitoring the activities of all the industries, industrialists

Started following statutory provisions seriously. By holding environmental values, they follow and obey environmental laws, do the work in the boundaries of all the rules and regulation as they come to know that if they ignore it for today, tomorrow nothing will be left to work with.

Even before, India's independence in 1947, several environmental legislation existed but the real impetus for bringing about well- developed framework came only after the UN conference on the Human Environment (Stockholm 1972) under the influence of this declaration, the national conference for environmental policy and planning within the department of science and technology set up in 1977. This council later evolved into full fledged ministry of environment and forests (MOEF) in 1985, which today is the apex administrative body in the country for regulating and ensuring environment protection.

After the Stockholm conference in 1976, constitution sanction was given to environmental concern through the 42nd amendment, which incorporated them into the directive principles of state policy and fundamental rights and duties.

Since 1970, an extensive network of environmental legislation has grown in the country. The pollution control boards (both-central pollution Control board CPCB and State pollution control board SPCB) together with MOEF from the regulatory and administrative core of the sector.

To develop and promote initiative for protection and improvement of Environment, a policy statement was brought out by MOEF in 1992. The main focus was on abatement of pollution and the national conservation strategy development.

The EAP (Environmental action programme) was formulated in 1993 with the objective of improving environmental services and integrating environmental considerations in to development programme. Our government has established some legal laws and regulation regarding environmental protection such as –

1. The Environment Protection Act (1986)

These rules lay down the procedures for setting standards of emission or discharge of environmental pollutions. The rules prescribe the parameters for the central government, under which it can issue orders of prohibition and restrictions on the location and operation of industries in different areas. The rules lay down the procedure for serving notice, taking samples, submission of samples for analysis and laboratory reports.

2. The Factories Act, 1948 and its Amendment in 1987

The factories act 1940 was a post independence state that explicitly showed concern for the environment, the primary aim of the 1948 act has been to ensure the welfare of workers not only in their working conditions in factories but also their employment benefits. While ensuring the safety and health of the worker, the Act contributes to environment protection.

The Act contains the list of 29 categories of industries including hazardous processes, which are defined as a process or activity where unless specific care is taken, raw material used therein, or the intermediate or the finished products –

- Cause material impairment to health of the persons engaged
- Result in pollution of the general environment.

3. Hazardous Wastes

There are no. of laws developed which directly or in directly deal with hazardous wastes like –

(*a*) Hazardous wastes (Management and Handling) Rules, 1989 — Which brought out a guidelines for manufacture, strong, and import of hazardous chemicals and for management of hazardous wastes.

(*b*) Municipal Wastes (Management and handling) rules 2000 — Whose aim to enable municipalities to dispose municipal solid wastes in scientific manner.

(*c*) Bio chemical wastes (Management and handling) rules 1998 - Were formulated along parallel lines for proper disposal, transport etc. of infectious wastage.

(*d*) Hazardous wastes (Management and handling) Amendment rules 2000 — A recent notification issued with the view of providing guidelines for the import and export of hazardous waste in the country.

4. Public liability Insurance Act (PLIA) 1991

The Act covers the accidents involving hazardous substances and insurance coverage for these. Where death or injury result from an accident, this act makes the owner liable to provide relief as is specified in the schedule of the Act. The PLIA was amended in 1992, and the central government was authorized to establish the Environmental Relief fund, for making relief payment.

5. National Environment Tribunal Act, 1995

The Act provided strict liability for damages arising out of any accident occurring while handling any hazardous substance and for the establishment of a National Environment Tribunal for effective and expeditious disposal of cases arising from such accident, with a view to give belief and compensation for damages to persons property and the environment and for the matters connected there with or incidental there to.

6. The National Environment Appellate Authority Act, 1997

The Act provided for the establishment of a national Environment Appellate Authority to hear appeals with respect to restriction of areas in which any industry operation or process or clears of industries, operation or processes could not cry out or would be allowed to carry out subject to certain safeguards under the Environment (Protection) Act, 1986.

14.6 SOME GRAVE EXAMPLES OF ENVIRONMENTAL POLLUTION

(A) *Bhopal Gas Tragedy*

On 3rd December 1984, in a highly populated city, Bhopal, Central India, poisonous vapor burst from the tall stakes of the union carbide pesticide plant isocyanate. This vapor was a highly toxic cloud of methyl. Around 800,000 people living in Bhopal at the time, 2000 died immediately, and as many as 300,000 were injured. In addition, about 7,000 animals were injured, of which about one thousand were killed.

The post accident analysis of the process showed that the accident started when a tank containing methyl isocyanate leaked. MIC is an extremely reactive chemical and is used in production of the insecticide carbaryl. 'The scientific reason for the accident at Bhopal is that water entered the tank where 40 cubic meters of MIC was started when water and MIC mixed, an exothermic reaction started, producing lot of heat. Because of increased pressure, the safety valve of the tank burst. About 20-30 tonnes of MIC were released during the have that the leak took place. The gas leaked from 30 metre high chimney and this height was not enough to reduce the effects of the discharge. The reason was that the high moisture content (aerosol) in the discharge when evaporating, gave risk to heavy gas which rapidly rank sank to the ground.

Numerous studies have been conducted on the incident and in most of the studies, the two main agencies analyzed were the union carbide corporation and Indian govt. one of the major reason for the tragedy was a result of a combinations of human factors and incorrectly designed safety system.

Union carbide itself believed that the tragedy resulted when a disgruntled plant employee, apparently bent on spoiling a batch of methyl isocyanides, added water to a storage tank. Some other experts in industrial safety believe that the tragedy was preventable and it was due to the negligence on the part of the union carbide corporation and its corporate subsidiary union carbide of India Ltd, which had the responsibility for taking care of the day-to-day operations of the facility. The corporation and its subsidiary were also charged with corporate irresponsibility for pursuing the profits instead of the safety and hazard standards.

The Indian government, in response to the tragedy and pressure from the Indian people, filed a compensation lawsuit against the UCC for an estimated 3 billion dollar; on the other hand, UCC strongly felt that the Indian govt. was to blame.

13 years later not much has changed. Union Carbide India Ltd is an abandoned site in Bhopal. In Oct. 1991 the Indian Supreme Court upheld a settlement which had been appealed from a lower court decision of 1989, under which union carbide had to pay and 470 million in compensation of all claims. Today, union carbide is a six billion dollar company whose world-wide sales% is increasing every financial year.

But any how Bhopal gas tragedy was one of the worst industrial disasters in history.

(B) *Exxon Valdez disaster*

In 1989, Alaska was hit with a major ecological when the super tanker Exxon Valdez over 11 million gallons of crude oil into prince William sound over 1000 miles of wilderness shoreline were damaged in what was the largest and most destructive oil spill in U.S.

history. A quarter million seabirds died along with more than 3000 sea others, harbor seals and killer whales.

The research conducted by US govt. scientists tells that the oil patches left from the 1989 Exxon Valdez spill are still releasing toxins that harm sea life.

Brenda Ballachey of the survey's Alaska Science center said, "Within that area, I think it's going to take a long time for that oil to be gone and for the effects to go away".

(C) Chernobyl accident

On (April 25-26) 1986 the world's worst nuclear power accident occurred at Chernobyl in the former USSR (now Ukraine). The Chernobyl nuclear power plant located 80 miles north of Kiev had 4 reactors where numerous safety procedures were disregarded. At 1.23 a.m. the chain reaction in the reactor become out of control creating explosions and a fire ball which blew off the reactor's heavy steel and concrete lid. This accident killed more than 30 people immediately, and as a result of the high radiation levels in the surroundings 20 mile radius, 135,000 people had to be evacuated.

The main causes of Chernobyl Accident were lack of a safety culture, design fault in the RBMK reactor, violation of procedure etc.

After the Chernobyl accident radioactive material was widely dispersed and was measurable and resulted in effects over a vast area. The effects have been felt all over practically the whole of the northern hemisphere.

SUMMARY

Environment is the sum total of natural resources and man-made resources. Environmental pollution has become havoc for the whole world. Seeing the present situation and anticipating about the dangers of the future, business firms started think about Environmental ethics. The main facets of environmental ethics are resolving the conflicts, intergenerational ethics and spiritual ethics. Indian approach toward Environmental issues is also changing.

QUESTIONS

1. Explain in detail the concept of environmental ethics and the facets of Environmental ethics.
2. "Pollution has become the first enemy of "man kind" discuss about all types of pollution and their impact on environment.
3. Write an essay on environment protection in India.

Chapter 15

Corruption and Ethics

- ***Introduction***
- ***Mechanism of Corruption***
- ***Causes of Corruption***
- ***Impact of Corruption***
- ***Corruption—An Ethical Involvement***
- ***Summary***
- ***Case study***

15.1 INTRODUCTION

Corruption–No body is unaware of this word. Whether it is a public sector or private entities, education institution, businessmen, politician, officials from Govt. or PSU'S, corruption has become an inherent characteristic of any field.

It is difficult to define corruption, it would be of any type but generally we divide it in two parts –

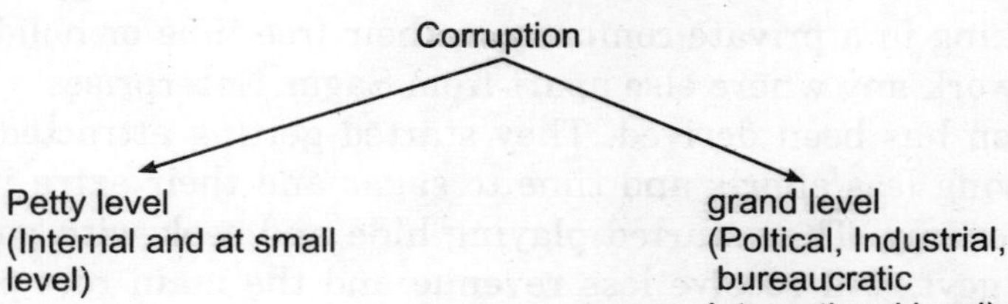

If we go by dictionary meaning of the word 'corruption', we find it is the misuse of public power for private gain. An event in which a person shows favour to another from whom he receives something with power and he misuses or abuses that power.

Some definitions are as follows –

- Corruption is the practice of unlawful or improper use of influence, power and other means. Political offices have been prone to corruption throughout history.
- Corruptness is the lack of integrity or honesty (especially susceptibility to bribery), use of position of trust for dishonest gain.
- Political corruption is the misuse of public office to provide gain. All forms of government are susceptible in practice to political corruptions which vary greatly from minor uses or influence and patronage to do and return favour, to institutionalized bribery and beyond.

  Though it is difficult to draw a clear cut line between grand corruption and petty corruption. Grand corruption is generally practiced by govt. officials, ministers, senior officials, where as petty corruption is attached with clerks, immigration officers and other low-paid servants.

  Petty corruption is a kind of removal of bureaucratic delays — paying people to do faster what they have already been paid to do, but grand corruption is usually international which is about the distortion of decision making in matters of economic significance.

15.2 MECHANISM OF CORRUPTION

When we find some corrupt activities within an organization (public/private) or out side the organization, it is tough to find how it occurs? What was the initial mode of this activity and whether there would be any terminal mode or not. How many people are involved in it and to which extent they are involved? All the questions are difficult to answer.

But then also we can say that when corruption comes in to any system, or working structure, that system or structure alone is not responsible for it to take place. It's like a cyclic theory of Algebra. It's a contribution of so many stakeholders, who are directly or indirectly attached with the system. To understand the cyclical theory we have to assume a hypothetical situation.

Mr. X and Mr. Y work in PSU Company — 'Sagar Enterprises'. The problem with these employees is inadequate and late payment. Even govt is unable to meet their expectations because of lack of funds. So to earn some extra money, Mr. X and Mr. Y both have started working in a private company in their free time or holidays, though it was not permitted to work any where else apart from Sagar Enterprises. Very soon their problem of solution has been derived. They started getting attracted more towards the new company, giving less efforts and time to sagar and their extra income because the part of hidden economy. They started playing hide and seek with govt. officials for tax concern so again govt. will receive less revenue and the main root problem of late and inadequate payment would remain as it is.

As we have seen in the above situation, when corruption starts at one end, automatically it effects other actions, as govt. was not having enough funds to pay the Sagar's employees on time. It also shows that some where in the underground, some corruption is going on so openly that govt is having no funds to pay, but from inside they do involve in corrupt practices. This kind of level of corruption is petty corruption so here we define corruption like —

"Corruption is the one which may influence the action of any person by offering, giving, and acceptance of any reward or inducement".

Most people believe that a small bribe is a victimless crime — wrong in principle but the sort of thing that is always going to happen in real world. Petty corruption hits the most vulnerable members of society hardest for example, the parents who can not afford to give gifts to head teacher or provide free medicines to doctor or the job hunters who can not arrange a 'fee' to pay to the official in charge of hiring.

Some times we find that entertainment and small gifts become issue of petty corruption. The kind of gift would be the deciding one whether it is under corruption or not. In how much frequency the gifts are given, what are their timings and value and most important whether reciprocity is these or it is only from one side.

Grand corruption is usually international because of its scale. When any bribe is paid, it is of course in the interest of both buyer and the receiver of a bribe. They both want to conceal as far as possible. When corruption takes place at international level, the payer of bribes are generally large companies operating in many countries, so they always try to keep themselves far away from any questionable transactions and simultaneously the recipient of a bribe will not want any details to be known.

For example –

(*a*) Medicines should be provided free of costs in free hospitals, but always the staff talks about having no stock. But the fact is that the medicines are transferred to nearby medical shops and doctors again prescribe the same drugs with the name of the medical store. Again some more margin!

(*b*) Buying a cinema ticket in 'black' directly from its owner whose intention is to cheat on the entertainment tax.

(*c*) A director of business school pays Rs. 5 lakh to a well known magazine for publishing an article praising the institute this should be done from a well regarded journalist, the payment will be made by cheques based on several such deals. The manager who arranges it gets an attractive commission.

15.3 CAUSES OF CORRUPTION

Corruption is not an easy issue to understand, to find causes behind it. There will always be grey areas and borderline cases. The reasons behind the origin and growth of corruption are hard to identify sometimes they are visible, sometimes hidden, sometimes situational while sometimes occasional.

As ' Corruption occurs where lack of integrity and honesty present, when people use their position and power for dishonest gain'.

- Corruption is indictments (as of public official by improper means as bribery) to violate duty (as by committing a felony); "he was held on charges of corruption and racketeering".

  (Source: logsci brineeton edu./cgibin/webwn 2.1)

- **Corruption in politics is having some different picture through out the history around the globe; political offices have been susceptible to corruption. Degree of corruption varies greatly from minor uses, influences or bribery to institutionalised delivery, practice of unlawful or improper use of influence, power and other means. In the broader terms the causes of corruption can be divided into two parts –**

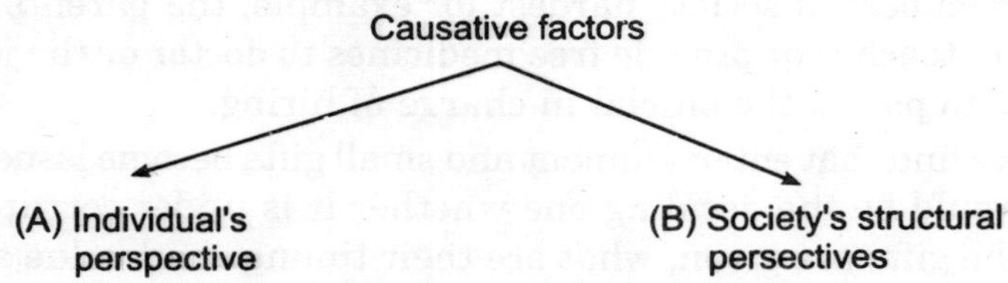

(*A*) Individual's Perspective

It explains the basic motivation of corruption is greediness like people want to get more money with less efforts, they want to save money by paying less tax. They want to enjoy unfair advantages over others.

This perspective view corruption as the inability to withstand temptation like politician to save their position, employees try to earn extra money from other source to maintain their standard of living.

(*B*) Society's Structural Perspectives

It views the origin of corruption because of various political, social cultural needs of the society. Corruption develops in the structure where the risk of being caught is far less than the reward of being corrupt. In general the basic factors behind corruption can be -

1. **Culture – At broad level culture comes into the picture, some activities and practices become gradually the culture of the society like gift culture in Africa where it has become a tradition to give gratuity/tip/gifts/rewards for services rendered. So any work can't be done without any reward or gift.**

   In some countries, in commercial segment of business, for each and every transaction whether small or big is to be accompanied by giving personal gifts and benefits.

2. **Inadequate, late and low salaries** – People find that it is very difficult to be and to stay honest, trustworthy and hardworking on a low and inadequate salary when they know that people who have lower talent, lower caliber than the honest ones in higher responsible positions, with corrupt practices earn high salaries and maintain high standard of life.

3. **Weak legal framework and absence of rules and regulations** – To organise people, steer them towards a common goal, unite them to make them ensue that every one is treated fairly; all the organizations must have proper regulations, rules, policies which must be communicated well.

Similarly each and every country must have a strong legal framework that manage and guide all its citizens. Corruption develops in countries where laws, rules and regulations are there but only in writing form, practically the applications of these is very poor and the organization where proper channel and framework of code of conduct, code of ethics have not been developed.

4. **The adherence to transparency and accountability is nil** – The principles of transparency and accountability are the prerequisites for democracy in the presence of transparency, a surety of preserved the right to freedom of speech, transparent role of govt. officers, Civil servants such as media and inform to people about right and wrong (both) doing of these staff where as presence of principle of accountability finds officers are accountable for what ever they do, they be very ready to give reasons, explanation behind their actions and decisions to the public corruption flourishes where there is no transparency in the organization and it finds futile in the situation where lack of effective institutional mechanism is developed and in absence of account ability.
5. **Other Reasons** – There are some other reasons like –
   (*a*) Opportunities– Some opportunistic people are of that kind whenever opportunity knocks the door they happily grab it, make use of it corruptly.
   (*b*) Circumstances – In some circumstances, people become helpless and they become the puppets in the hands of unwanted corruption.
   (*c*) International Phenomenon– People say that its on global scale, now it is just common, every body does it then why we not.

Corruption around the globe –

Corruption is universal phenomenon; it is not restricted to south zone or north zone, not limited to us or U.K. It is every where as because the birth place of corruption is human mind so it exists every where.

Corruption in Asia –

According to a survey report conducted by some foreign business executives, India and Indonesia are the worst and Singapore is the least corrupt country in Asia. India's position as against the whole world is ranked among the 30 most corrupt nations with a score of 2.7 on a scale of 10.

Corruption in less developed countries –

Corruption is a more serious matter in LDCs. The conditions of these countries are such that corruption is likely to have different causes and consequences than in more developed countries. As the socio-economic conditions are very pathetic in this country which causes the growth of corruption. Corruption is the symptom of deep-rooted economic and political weaknesses and short comings in the legislative and judicial system of the country. First of all, the chances of being caught while corrupt activities are small and if the penalties when caught are light. Non Government organizations that could serve as watch dogs and provide information on corrupt practices are generally not well developed.

15.4 IMPACT OF CORRUPTION

As corruption is an abuse of public office for private gain and it is often symptomatic of wider governance problems hurting economic development so the impacts of corruption are also very dangerous some are as follows –

1. *It slows economic development –*

   It reduces revenues in the form of taxes, customs.

   It increases cost of contracts. It leads to delays as officials are behind the bigger bribes. Quality of work cannot be maintained. Decisions are based more on expected individual gain than by society's needs.
2. *It reduces investment –*

   Corruption is having direct link with investment. Acc. to World Bank Report, 1997–98, a country's ratio of gross investment/GDP is reduced by 32% of corruption is perceived as high.
3. *It increases poverty –*

   When political power is translated corruptly into economic gains, corruption redistributes resources from the poor to the rich.
4. *It leads to poor administration –*

   If the officials are appointed because of some contacts or links they will not be motivated and as competent as they should.
5. *Decline in human development –*

   Corruption brings too much uncertainty and high transaction costs. It dissuades innovation and long term planning. People who started enjoying corrupt activities forget about their own development as well as they never contribute to organizations growth.
6. *It increases discrimination and unfair treatment.*
7. It supports criminal activities as judges and police are bribed by smugglers. It makes societies unsafe.
8. It distorts incentives and creates uncertainties about the expected profits of productive activities. Hence, corruption can undermine the functioning of countries and lower the efficiency of production having a destructive impact on a country's economic and political system.

15.5 CORRUPTION – AN ETHICAL INVOLVEMENT

(*A*) Is Corruption a Value Maximizing Strategy?

The Significance of business ethics in the development of economics is remarkable. Though ethical behaviour, following ethical norms could be costly but the results of ignoring ethics conformly costlier. The other side of economy is corruption, which induces less optional policies in society and large adverse effects on social welfare.

The list of eco-socio obligation of a private firm is becoming longer and longer. So they must give maximum return to their stakeholder by maximizing profits.

Therefore to fulfill these objectives companies use corrupt activities like paying bribes to get favored treatment, concessions.

Companies justify these kinds of routine activities and behaviors as means to their greater goal of the creation of economic value and return on investment.

(*B*) Corruption Involves Both Buyer and Seller

Corruption is kind of deal in which buyer and seller both take part, equally. It at any one end, one denies, it would not occur, so to reduce it, the co-operation of both of the parties are required.

(*C*) Privatization and Corruption

Is it possible to reduce corruption by introducing privatization in the economic structure? Yes, to some extent it can be, as it transfers the owners from public to private, remove certain assets from state control and convert them into private market driven hands, but the darker side is because of privatization the corruption practices are becoming deeper and stronger, the private owned companies have increased the magnitude of corruption which crossed all the limits as they only bother about their profits and image.

For example, when privatization of public enterprises in Peru occurred, it curtailed the levels of corruption in the Public sector but the by-products which has given was the lack of transparency, accountability, increased corrupt activities.

(*D*) Corruption and Law

As we know that corruption involves both buyer and a seller and their co-operation is needed to make a serious reduction in corruption possible.

Company is a creation of law operating in multiple political jurisdictions only with the permission of governments and its creation is justified in so far as it, on balance, further, desirable, social goals both economic and political so the need of the hour is that managers, and directors need to establish clear and well-enforced corporate guidelines and policies against corruption rather than they rely on the personal morality of employees.

Organizations should not be anthropomorphized regarding rights and responsibilities, but still have moral responsibilities and can not always be reduced to individual responsibilities. Donaldson in 1989 presented this view that citizens accept organizations the benefits increased productivity outweighed the costs. Organizations shows some conduct that destabilize the market producing inefficient results and therefore, laws exist to contain the worst sorts of behavior such as fraud against customers, requiring certain types of information disclosure and control.

As a company is a receiver and recipient of the market system and the normative justification of market rests on their efficiency and so a company has an obligation to act in ways that improve the efficient functioning of the market otherwise the entire market system leaves itself open to charges of immorality and illegitimacy. Not, only corruption affects the power and capacity of honest entrepreneurs to carry out their activities but also it erodes public confidence in the market. So the company has a duty not only to refuse corrupt demands but also make these corrupt demands to public.

Some companies use corruption as good means to achieve their desired ends. As companies are dependent for their success not only on the existence of a functioning market system but also on a state that facilitates market activity and maintains order and stability.

If we talk about corruption in globalization 'Hazler and Sullivan' 1994 have suggested that Transnational corruption, or the bribery of government officials by foreign business interest is harmful to national economic and political systems, particularly within those countries that host the corrupt practices promoting financial incompetence by adding an extra and unwarranted level of cost to routine government functions and undermining governmental legitimacy by damaging public confidence in the national administration. So any how transnational corruption has had a destructive impact globally by bringing inefficiency to national economics.

Therefore, the companies that are leaders in their industries or are major international actors have a particular strong obligation to take a public anti corruption stand.

SUMMARY

Corruption has now become a universal phenomenon. The various causes of corruption are circumstances, greediness, misconception etc. It is very clear that the origin of corruptions is human mind. The consequences of corruption are always dangerous to society like it slows development, it hurts people, it makes societies unsafe etc. At the end of the chapter, the interlink between Ethics and corruption has been explained with some preventive steps to control the corruption.

QUESTIONS

1. What do you mean by corruption? How does it take place?
2. "India ranks among the most corrupted nations". Comment on it.
3. Explain in detail the causes and consequences of corruption.
4. Explain the interlinked between ethics and corruption law and corruption.

CASE STUDY

"Chennai Cement Ltd". was market leader (CCL)–It used to supply cement in Tamilnadu, Andhra Pradesh and Kerala. This company is marketing in southern states since 60 years, successfully enjoying sort of monopoly. The important thing here is their major portion of sales was towards govt. supply.

However, recently the company started losing its market share of govt. supply to their competitor because of some activities of the competitors like giving bribes to obtain big orders of govt. supply.

Chennai Cement Ltd. Being a traditional company has been known in the market for its ethical practices and providing good services to its customers. The company always cared for its employer, small contractors, distributors and customers. CCL's recent worry about losing customers and it's limitation to diversify the target market because of limited staff.

Therefore, now the big question in front of CCL is how to control the corrupt practices of the competitors and retain its share of the govt. sector being ethical!

Chapter 16

Ethical Issues: Gender Ethics, Sexual Harassment and Discrimination

- ***Introduction***
- ***Discrimination***
- ***Nature of Discrimination***
- ***Sexual Harassment***
- ***Gender Ethics***
- ***Feminist Ethics***
- ***Summary***
- ***Case Study***

16.1 INTRODUCTION

As discussed in earlier chapter ethics plays quite an important role in all the management field like marketing, finance, HRM, IT etc. But looking forward towards some latest, more radical approaches like discrimination, gender ethics, feminist ethics, sexual harassment at work place, we find that these field are also having involvement of ethics.

16.2 DISCRIMINATION

India being a democratic country has always provided freedom and rights to pursue opportunity. As per the policies, laws, legal rules & regulation there is no kind of discrimination on the basis of gender, caste or race. But the real and actual scene is different. So many people have been target of economic discrimination.

16.3 NATURE OF DISCRIMINATION

- Original meaning of the term: "to distinguish one object from another".
- Acquired judgmental connotations –
  - Unfair distinctions underwriting unjust treatment "the wrongful act of distinguishing illicitly among people not on the basis of individuals merit but on the basis of prejudice or some other morally invidious attitude".
  - Women (sexism)
  - African - American (racial discrimination)
  - The disabled
  - Hispanics, Asians, Native Americans.

Discrimination in Employment

Three elements: a decision towards one or more (Prospective) employees.

1. that is not based on individual merit –
   - Seniority and experience
   - Educational qualifications and job performance ratings.
2. That derives from some morally unjustified attitude –
   - Such as racial or sexual prejudice
   - False stereotypes
3. That has a harmful or negative impact on the interest of the employees–
   - Jobs
   - Pay
   - Promotions.

Past and Present Victims of Discrimination

- Religious groups: Catholic Jews
- Ethnic groups: Italians, Poles, Irish
- Racial groups: African, Americans, Hispanics, Asians.

India is not the single nation where we find the discriminations exists. For ex. Japan, One of the most developed nation of the world, still favours men over women and emphatic gender inequality in business organization.

The development and advances in gender equality and no discrimination are speeding up in some countries like USA, Denmark, Sweden are we some examples where reforms, laws are establishing to give equal treatment to females.

USA has been protecting its citizen from economic discrimination with suitable laws. For example, US civil rights act of 1964 (Title VII) provides protection in the following area —

- Race
- National origin

- Disabilities
- Colour
- Religion
- Sex
- Age

Subtle discrimination does exist in the professional work place. If we come to know the facts about it, we might get the key to overcome the obstacles of cultural differences and to successfully integrate at all levels of the corporate world. Whether it is a problem of human rights or equality or any other, discrimination in any sense of word is unfair and may infringe on the right of individual to pursue their own goals and their own way of life.

16.4 SEXUAL HARASSMENT

Sexual harassment is –

- A kind of discrimination directed primarily at women.
- Difficult to define and hence to police and prevent.
- Equal employment opportunity commission (EEOC) 1978 guidelines about sexual harassment –

  It include unwelcome sexual advances and request for sexual favours and other verbal or physical contact of a sexual nature.

  In short sexual harassment is an unwanted activity of a sexual nature that affects an individual's employment.

  The issue of sexual harassment got increasing attention by corporation and media in the 1980's, because of the growing ranks of the female employees.

It may include –

- Remarks
- Looks
- Touching
- Jokes
- Attitudes
- Sexual comments
- Recurring requests for dates
- Use of sexual artifacts
- Use of sexual explicit language.

Many organizations have relieved the cost of sexual harassment like (the very talented employees proved to be important assets left the job, because of sexually harassment, or else some employees could not focus attention to their jobs etc.)

The problem of sexual harassment is growing like a mushroom around the world. ILO's study on violence at work place shows that it is a very big and serious matter. The incidences of sexual harassment noted in European countries are like—

Netherlands– 53%, Spain– 40%, UK– 73%, Germany– 93%, Norway– 41%.

But in last few years organizations have made considerable progress towards limiting over to forms of sexual harassments of female employees. The problems today are more subtle norms of sexual harassment. The topic of sexual harassment is about power. It seems correct whether the harassment comes from a supervisor, boss, co-worker or any employee. If we look at first supervisor - employee relations. The supervisor has the power with which he assigns the work to the employee, monitor the work, evaluate the performance, and make recommendations for salary increment and promotion.

The employees want favorable performance review from the supervisors end. And the powerful supervisor starts using his rights and powers in wrong manner, harassing female employees. The sexually harassed employees are afraid of speaking out for fear of retaliation by the supervisor. Also if any one collects the courage to complain, whether there are witnesses about the happenings, also if other who has been harassed will come forth?

In some organization we find co-workers also use their influence to sexually harass peers. Though they don't have power position, but they have information, their support and co-operation which in any case is required while working in teams. So in any situation sexual harassment is illegal. It's about an individual controlling or threatening others.

Any how, women must have protection from unwelcome attention at the work place which could undermine their career prospecting. To prevent sexual harassment at work place, some policies, laws should be developed. The companies should follow the following guidelines to prevent the same from occurring.

- Strong and effective company policies to be formulated.
- Company's policies should be enforced.
- Communicating the policy to all the members of the organization.
- Setting up a procedure for reporting violations.
- Taking appropriate actions.

Supreme Court in India has issued certain guidelines for this and legislation on sexual harassment at work has also been drafted in India. The will, which does not cover women of Jammu and Kashmir, applies to all forms of work, from agricultural labour to the IT sector. Any establishment with 50 or more employees is supposed to setup an internal complaints committee of three members of whom at least two must be women. There has to be an external experts committee to look into complaints of which half the members have to be women.

But the problem with the bill is it says nothing about it the harassment takes place at educational institutions (like if one student harasses another). There are some instances where people have brought false charges against colleagues or superiors with modified intentions. The bill also says nothing about any preventive steps.

So in short, we can say that a more tender sensitive legal system will encourage women to come forward with their grievances. Instead of searching for the single solution, depending upon laws and legislation, some other voluntarily practices should be started in organizations like —

- Each and every cause which lead to sexual harassment should be analyzed, intervention strategies to be executed.

16.5 GENDER ETHICS

The simple meaning of gender ethics is that men and women should be treated as equals. To treat them differently would be unethical. The equality between them must be reinforced by laws and regulations.

Gender ethics is much wider than simply job discrimination, wages inequality etc. though we find that discrimination in remuneration between men and women is seen and present every where in India, Where female wages rate are very less than those of males. Though Equal Remuneration Act is made but it is inadequate in its scope for preventing the exploitation of female employees.

Therefore we find that gender ethics involves mainly the equality between men and women and for this, organizational policies should be similarly fashioned. And if any organization is violating this principle it must be punished. Women must fight for their rights

Some decades ago, the condition of women in India was very different. They used to be considered as always dependent —

"In childhood a women should be in her father's control, in youth in her husband's and if he dies in her sons"– *Manusmriti*

But fortunately with the effective and proper guidance of some great leaders, the condition of Indian women started improving regarding respect, protection, security and independence.

16.6 FEMINIST ETHICS

In this development a new concept has initiated 'Feminist Ethics' – It is an attempt to revise, reformulate or rethink those aspects of traditional ethics that depreciate or devalue women's moral experience. A famous feminist philosopher 'Alison Jagar' finds some limitations in traditional western ethics for women –

1. It slows little concern for women's as compared to men's interests and rights.
2. It suggests that, on the average, women are not as morally developed as men.
3. It over values a culturally masculine trait like independence, autonomous, separation etc. and undervalues culturally feminine traits like interdependence, community, emotion, peace etc.
4. It favors culturally masculine ways of moral reasoning that emphasize rules universality and impartiality ever culturally feminine ways of moral reasoning that emphasize relation ships particularity and partiality.

   Like Jagar, other feminist also have developed a wide variety of women - centered approaches to ethics which highlights the difference between men's and women's respective situation in life - biological and social, provides strategies for dealing with issues that arise in private as well as public life and offers suggestions and actions relatively.

   So the overall given to discuss about gender ethics is to create a moral theory that generate non-sexist moral principles, policies and practices.

SUMMARY

Discrimination, whether on the basis of gender, caste or race is always unethical. USA and other western countries as well as India have provided many laws and regulation to provide protection to minorities against discrimination but subtle discrimination has become part and parcel of work places. The practice of sexual harassment at work place is also seen here and there. Organization must understand their responsibilities to prevent it by establishing programmers which deal with sexual harassment on the job. Gender ethics is the branch of ethics which says that male and female must be treated equal.

QUESTIONS

1. Explain the term discrimination why is job discrimination found.
2. Sexual harassment is becoming dominant in certain type of industries. Explain the preventive steps to deal with this problem.
3. What is gender ethics and how for it has been implemented in work force?

CASE STUDY

John and George have been employed by an American company, at the same position. Both were asked to report to Mr. Bill Cruise, Head of marketing dept. while John was white American, George was African American.

Both were invited along with the other employees of the same organization by Mr. Cruise for Saturday night party, which was held on weekly basis.

George felt uncomfortable at the party because he was the only minority out of 8-10 employees with their families present over there. While John was quite comfortable at the party and soon developed good relations with every body, including Mr. Cruise. for Saturday night party, this was held on weekly basis.

Mr. George, subsequently, stopped going to these parties and always found some excuses for not being able to attend the party.

After 6 months, Mr. John was promoted, while Mr. George remained at the same position, because John was maintaining good relations with his boss, Mr. Cruise had recommended John's name to the management for promotion.

Here George felt, that he too deserved the promotion because, he too was efficient in his work and compared himself equal if not more than John. A new recruitment, Henry (A white American) came as a replacement with Mr. Cruise in a matter of one month. George became concerned as the new person was following foot steps of John

What should George do?

References

1. *Ethics in Management* — S.A. Sherlekar.
2. *Business Ethics* — C.S.V. Murthy, Himalaya Publishing House.
3. *Business Ethics and Mnagerial Values* – S.K. Bhatia.
4. *A Study in Business Ethics* — Rituparana Raj.
5. *Time of India* — Ascent (May 11, 2005).
6. *Case Study and Case Problem in Management* — Dr. Arvind Shukla.
7. *Case Sudies in Indian Management* — Dr. M.A. Rohok.
8. *Cases in Management* — Girish Pannalal Jakhotiya and Manjiri G. Jakhotiya.
9. *Ethics, Indian Ethos and Management* — S. Balachandran, K.C.R. Raja, B.K. Nair.
10. HRM Review, April 2005, ICFAI University Press.
11. Times of India (18.7.05) — Article on Toothless Bill (Legalisation on Sexual Harassment at Work Introduced).
12. The Economic Times online.